Immigratio⁓ ⁓⁓h⁓
and raci⁓

This textbook provides the first wide-ranging and accessible examination of the issues of immigration, ethnicity and racism in Britain
during the years 1815–1945. The study covers a fascinating period
in the history of these developments in British Society, from the
Irish immigration of the early nineteenth century to the eve of the
post-war influxes. The book's span, encompassing all of the major
groups making their way into Britain, and its conciseness, make it
the ideal introductory text for students.

The book tackles four basic themes. First, the author explores
why so many immigrants made their way to Britain during the
years 1815–1945. Second, the study deals with the geographical,
gender and economic divisions of the newcomers. Third, it ad-
dresses the topic of ethnicity, focusing upon a wide range of issues,
including religious, philanthropic, educational, social and political
activities. Finally, the volume tackles the reactions of British society
to the newcomers.

Panikos Panayi brings together the results of extensive and up-
to-date research in this succinct study. The range of sources used
and the lively and clear analysis makes this book suitable for a
readership ranging from the student and general reader to the
specialist in modern British History.

NEW FRONTIERS IN HISTORY

series editors

Mark Greengrass
Department of History, Sheffield University

John Stevenson
Worcester College, Oxford

This important new series reflects the substantial expansion that has occurred in the scope of history syllabuses. As new subject areas have emerged and syllabuses have come to focus more upon methods of historical enquiry and knowledge of source materials, a growing need has arisen for correspondingly broad-ranging textbooks.

New Frontiers in History provides up-to-date overviews of key topics in British, European and world history, together with accompanying source material and appendices. Authors focus upon subjects where revisionist work is being undertaken, providing a fresh viewpoint which will be welcomed by students and sixth-formers. The series also explores established topics which have attracted much conflicting analysis and require a synthesis of the state of the debate.

Published Titles

C. J. Bartlett   Defence and diplomacy: Britain and the Great Powers, 1815–1914

Jeremy Black   The politics of Britain, 1688–1800

Keith Laybourn   The General Strike of 1926

Daniel Szechi   The Jacobites: Britain and Europe, 1688–1788

Forthcoming titles

Paul Bookbinder   The Weimar Republic

Joanna Bourke   Production and reproduction: working women in Britain, 1860–1960

Michael Braddick   The nerves of state: taxation and the financing of the English state, 1558–1714

Ciaran Brady   The unplanned conquest: social changes and political conflict in sixteenth-century Ireland

David Brooks   The age of upheaval: Edwardian politics, 1899–1914

David Carlton   Churchill and the Soviets

Carl Chinn   Poverty and the urban poor in the nineteenth century

Barry Coward   The Cromwellian Protectorate

Conan Fischer   The rise of the Nazis

Neville Kirk   The rise of Labour, 1850–1920

Tony Kushner   The Holocaust and its aftermath

Alan O'Day   Irish Home Rule

John Whittam   Fascist Italy

Immigration, ethnicity and racism in Britain, 1815–1945

Panikos Panayi

Manchester University Press

Manchester and New York

Distributed exclusively in the USA and Canada by St. Martin's Press

Copyright © Panikos Panayi 1994

Published by Manchester University Press
Oxford Road, Manchester M13 9NR, UK
and Room 400, 175 Fifth Avenue, New York, NY 10010, USA

Distributed exclusively in the USA and Canada by St. Martin's Press, Inc.,
175 Fifth Avenue, New York, NY 10010, USA

British Library Cataloguing-in-Publication Data
A catalogue record for this book is available from the British Library

Library of Congress Cataloging-in-Publication Data
Panayi, Panikos.
  Immigration, ethnicity, and racism in Britain, 1815–1945 / Panikos
Panayi.
    p. cm. — (New frontiers in history)
  Includes bibliographical references.
  ISBN 0–7190–3697–6 (hard). — ISBN 0–7190–3698–4 (paper)
  1. Great Britain—Emigration and immigration—History.
2. Immigrants—Great Britain—History. 3. Minorities—Great
Britain—History. 4. Ethnicity—Great Britain—History. 5. Racism–
–Great Britain—History. I. Title. II. Series.
JV7624.P36 1994
305.8'00941—dc20   93–49041

ISBN 0 7190 3697 6 *hardback*
     0 7190 3698 4 *paperback*

Typeset by The Midlands Book Typesetting Company, Loughborough
Printed in Great Britain by Bell and Bain Ltd, Glasgow

275849

Contents

Acknowledgement

The research for this volume was made possible by a grant from the Nuffield Foundation, which I gratefully acknowledge.

To all the students I have enjoyed teaching at the start of my career.

Introduction

Despite the root and branch impact of immigrant minorities on British society, particularly since the end of the Second World War, the present study represents only the fourth general history of immigrants in Britain over any length of time. The others consist of William Cunningham's *Alien Immigrants to England*, originally published in 1897, and, more recently, Jim Walvin's *Passage to Britain*, and Colin Holmes's *John Bull's Island*.[1] The books by Cunningham and Holmes represent landmarks, especially the latter, while that by Walvin is more limited.

However, despite the lack of general studies, immigration history has finally taken off in Britain during the last decade, despite its relatively late start as a field of study in comparison with the United States, or in comparison with other aspects of 'history from below', such as women's history and working class history. While it may still not have established itself in quite the same way as the last two themes, a substantial number of books and articles appear every year on the subject of immigrants in British history from medieval times to the present.

Nevertheless, publications tend to concentrate on particular minorities and themes. With regard to the former, three groups have received particular attention. The first of these consists of Jews, whose historiography began to take shape during the mid-nineteenth century with the publication of two substantial books,[2] followed by further volumes in the early twentieth century, and continued by a series of scholars, notably Cecil Roth and V. D. Lipman, until the present, when a series of prolific scholars,

1

notably Geoffrey Alderman, Tony Kushner and David Cesarani, have led the way. We can make similar comments about Irish historiography, which begins in the late nineteenth century,[3] although it declines in the early twentieth century, to revive from the 1940s and, more especially, the 1980s.[4] The history of Black people has also received a fair amount of attention, although this did not take off until the 1970s, since when numerous books and articles have appeared.[5]

But apart from these three groups, other minorities remain understudied. Italians[6] and Germans[7] did not begin to receive serious attention until the 1980s. In the case of the latter this remains especially surprising as they represented the largest group in Britain, after the Irish, until 1891. The history of other minorities, such as Poles, Greeks and Lithuanians, has received patchy attention, while some groups have had virtually no work carried out upon them at all, including post-Huguenot French immigrants, Spaniards and Chinese.

As well as the above gaps in the study of specific minorities, we can also point to a concentration upon particular themes within British immigration history, to the exclusion of others. In the first place, we can mention the lack of attention to the process and mechanics of immigration. A few exceptions exist in this context, notably on the Irish movement to Britain during the mid-nineteenth century. Second, the history of ethnicity, of the lives of the immigrants, their social institutions, churches and clubs has tended to be ignored, although this does not represent as large a gap as that on the immigration process.

The main focus in the history of minorities in Britain has been upon newcomers as victims. We can make this point especially about the work of Colin Holmes,[8] but we can further point to the large numbers of books on, for instance, the internment episode during the Second World War.[9] My own previous work has also focused upon immigrants as victims.[10] We must continue to welcome the appearance of further similar studies because they form part of a reinterpretation of British history which questions Britain's liberal traditions. But while every immigrant grouping in British history has faced hostility, which has always manifested itself in violence, the history of immigrant groups is more complex than simply the negative reactions of British society towards them. Feelings towards newcomers also manifest themselves positively.

Introduction

The present study provides an introductory survey of the history of minorities in the period 1815–1945, from the eve of the massive Irish influx to the eve of the still larger immigration of people from the British Empire and Commonwealth. In addition, this book also aims to set an agenda for the study of immigration history, not just within Britain, but also internationally. The present study is not a comprehensive empirical survey, in the nature of Holmes's *John Bull's Island*. Instead, the book takes a thematic approach, tackling four issues: first, the reasons for, and process of, migration; second, the structure of the immigrant communities; third, ethnicity; and, fourth, reactions towards newcomers. However, before this, a brief chapter introduces the immigration of minorities to Britain before 1815. The purpose of this section lies in tracing those groups who made their way to Britain before the early nineteenth century, as well as demonstrating the importance of these earlier movements and settlements for the subsequent development of the major immigrant groups to Britain, especially the Irish, Germans and Jews. In the case of the last two especially, we can see a continuity in areas of residence.

As mentioned above, the book has four main thematic chapters. In order to understand the first of these, we have to appreciate the extreme complexity of population movements to nineteenth century Britain. We cannot accept a straightforward Marxist theory put forward effectively by Dirk Hoerder[11] for the nineteenth century European economy and by, amongst others, Stephen Castles[12] for post-war Europe. These ideas, which see immigration following booms in capitalist economies, cannot work for nineteenth century Britain, both because it represented a country of net emigration and because, in comparison with the United States, the economy was too small to suck in millions of immigrants during a cyclical boom of capitalism. Furthermore, England, Scotland and Wales could use their own expanding population as fodder for the industrialisation process.

While not dismissing the Marxist interpretations of population movement, my own ideas on immigration to Britain from 1815 to 1945 function with the use of a more sophisticated, but seemingly traditional, theory to which push, pull and enabling factors all contribute. Furthermore, we also have to recognise the existence of underlying, medium term and personal factors, as well as differentiating between political refugees and economic immigrants.

Push factors included, in the case of underlying ones, population growth and, in many cases, an autocratic political system; while in the medium term we can include economic crises such as that which hit Europe in the second half of the 1840s, and periods of repression such as that which affected Germany after the failure of the 1848 revolution, or Russia under Tsars Alexander III and Nicholas II. The major enabling factor was the development of shipping during the course of the nineteenth century, which proved fundamental, not only for bringing immigrants to Britain but also for transporting transmigrants through the country, some of whom stayed. Pull factors consist of: in the case of the deepest, underlying ones, British immigration policy and the advanced state of the British economy in comparison with the countries from which immigrants originated; medium term pull factors include the state of the British economy; while personal ones revolve around representatives of the same family or, in the case of refugees, of the same political grouping, already residing in England, resulting in chain migration.

The second major objective of the present study is to establish the structure of immigrant groups in Britain during the period 1815–1945. This incorporates residential, age, gender and socio-economic distribution. Theoretical perspectives on these issues prove difficult to establish, but we can make a series of generalisations which hold together fairly well. With regard to geographical concentration, the major area of settlement was usually London, although exceptions exist to this rule, as in the case of Lithuanian and Chinese immigrants in the early decades of the twentieth century. Most minorities focused upon the capital also have concentrations outside London. In all cases, for reasons of prejudice against them in housing and because of the desire to maintain ethnic solidarity, minorities cluster in specific areas within cities and usually within particular streets. In London, while the East End has acted as a particular focus for many minorites, other areas have also attracted newcomers.

With regard to age and gender we have great difficulties in establishing patterns and this tends to depend on the size of communities, as well as the reasons for their settlement within Britain. Smaller groups tend to consist of adult males who marry outside their community, while larger ones, notably the nineteenth century Russian Jews and Irish, have a more balanced age and sex structure because of family migration.

4

Socio-economic distribution again varies, but we need to emphasise that a homogenous group hardly ever exists. In the case of most minorities, notwithstanding their size, a clear social structure exists, corresponding to, but usually ethnically distinct from, that of British society, ranging, in the case of larger minorities, from an underclass, through the working classes and various strands of middle classes, to, in some cases, an aristocracy. Within such a socio-economic structure, the range of occupations can vary enormously, although in most cases a focus develops upon a small number of occupations, particularly, though not exclusively, for those lower down the social scale.

After establishing the structure of immigrant communities in Britain between 1815 and 1945, the book then moves on to discuss ethnicity, a theme ignored by Holmes and Walvin, but one which US historians examined as early as Oscar Handlin's *The Uprooted*.[13] We can define ethnicity as the way in which members of a national, racial or religious grouping maintain an identity with people of the same background in a variety of official and unofficial ways. The three main methods by which ethnicity survives consist of: residence patterns, whereby members of the same group reside together; marriage patterns, in which immigrants and their children marry within their own grouping; and religious and social activity. However, we must recognise that we should speak of ethnicities rather than of one ethnicity. Class, religion and area of origin play a major role in determining the section of the ethnic group with which an individual identifies himself. However, as well as ethnicities within an ethnicity, we can also identify an overall one that holds all members of a group together. We can further illustrate this by speaking of ethnicity from above and ethnicity from below.

The former essentially refers to the development of institutions either by prominent members of a minority for their countrymen or by members of native society or by both together. We might even see this as a form of social or perhaps racial control. The main instruments here are religion, education and philanthropy. They serve to hold together members of the same grouping, who, however, rarely have any contact with each other because the British class system is too powerful a structure to be broken down by ethnicity. While members of a minority in nineteenth and twentieth century Britain may be German, Italian, Greek or

5

Jewish, they are also underclass, working class, petty bourgeois, middle class or even upper class. As well as recognising official ethnicity, we also need to bear in mind an ethnicity which springs from below. This encompasses a variety of activities including politics, trade solidarity, purely social groupings, and, in some cases, even religion. Once again, the organisations established function within the British class system. Residence and, especially, marriage patterns also represent ethnicity from below.

The present study concludes by focusing upon the attitudes of British society towards newcomers. Part of the reaction depends upon underlying views towards the country of origin of a particular immigrant group, which determines, to a considerable extent, attitudes towards a particular group in Britain. Racial ideas play a fundamental role in the period 1815–1945, as do the diplomatic relations of Britain with other European countries.

While accepting that neutral or positive attitudes exist towards minorities, attention focuses upon negative manifestations towards immigrants, which divide into official and unofficial, each of which manifested themselves in a variety of ways. With regard to the first of these, we can first recognise the existence of a racial state in the form of a racist judiciary and police force, to which contemporary sociologists and political scientists pay particular attention, but whose presence proves difficult, though not impossible, to measure before 1945. The British state has also reacted against minorities by the introduction of legislation, especially in the form of immigration laws, but also by passing nationality Acts. Governments have also used deportation and, especially in times of crisis, relocation and internment.

Popular hostility towards minorities goes hand in hand with official racism and can manifest itself in a variety of ways: at its most basic level in the refusal to enter into economic or social intercourse with a member of a minority, by which is meant a shopkeeper's unwillingness to serve a member of a minority or a more widespread disinclination to socialise. Connected with this, trade union hostility has developed, as has discrimination in employment. Press animosity remains ever present, both in the use of stereotypes and in the development of anti-alien campaigns against particular minorities at particular times. Stereotypes can develop into conspiracy theories over a prolonged period or during a time of extreme stress such as war. Racialist and xenophobic

6

pressure groups and political parties existed in Britain throughout the period 1845–1945. Although they never seized power, some of them influenced government thinking. Racial violence has also affected all minorities in nineteenth and twentieth century Britain, varying from small scale attacks involving a few people to, on several occasions, nationwide riots in which tens of thousands of people participated.

The above thematic approach will illustrate the fundamental similarites in the movement and position of immigrant minorities within Britain, while accepting that no two groups have faced an identical experience. One of the main factors in differentiating how minorities fare consists of their size. Origins prove less important in the differentiation of experiences, as a comparison between Germans and Russian Jews would demonstrate. The thematic approach better assists in the making of comparisons as well as giving a definite structure to this book, in contrast to the relatively unstructured approaches of both Holmes and Walvin.

The sources for immigration history have rarely received systematic attention. As the books in the series of which this study forms a part have appendices of documents, we can briefly comment upon sources and immigration history. The first point to make is that the range of material remains endless, varying from the personal papers of government ministers, to newspapers, to the publications of ethnic groups, to church registers and census material. The explanation for the range of sources lies in the fact that the study of minorities represents an all-encompassing sub-discipline of history, transcending the boundaries of economic, social and political history. We can expand slightly.

With reference to the process of migration, documentation of particular value can include British government publications examining the reasons for movement, a fact also revealed by personal letters written by immigrants. Government documents further reveal the attitudes of the receiving society to immigration in the form of immigration legislation. Church records and census returns provide clues as to the areas of origin of immigrants. The most valuable sources for the migration process could consist of those in the country of origin of the immigrants, although language problems create difficulties in the use of such material for an English scholar. However, local newspapers in the country of origin can prove fundamental here, as can publications of emigration societies.

A similar range of British sources to those for the migration process also help to reveal the structure of immigrant communities once within Britain, as do other types of documentation. The observations of social investigators and other urban commentators further prove important here, notably those of Henry Mayhew and Charles Booth, though there exist countless other writings. Trade journals, published by both British and immigrant organisations, have a role to play in establishing employment patterns.

For ethnicity, the main documentation, in a primary source based study, would consist of the publications of immigrant organisations, including newspapers. Annual reports of such bodies, including places of worship, trade unions and social clubs, represent a more important source, providing figures about the participation of members of a community in the activities of their ethnic group. Census returns prove fundamentally important in establishing residence and marriage patterns.

An endless range of documentation exists for measuring racism. For official manifestations we can point, for instance, to the papers of government departments, especially the Home Office, as well as parliamentary debates. Newspapers prove fundamental in measuring unofficial racism, not simply in the fact that they reveal their own racism, but also because they provide crucial information on racial violence and racist groupings. The publications of the latter also reveal information about them.

The present study samples primary sources but essentially represents a synthesis of secondary material published from the mid-nineteenth century. It is intended for students and scholars of British immigration history as well as the general reader. It aims to make an impact upon the study of the subject through its breakdown of immigration history into its logical component parts. Only this method can reveal the *whole* experience of immigrants in Britain.

Notes

1 William Cunningham, *Alien Immigrants to England*, London, 1897; James Walvin, *Passage to Britain: Immigration in British History and Politics*, Harmondsworth, 1984; Colin Holmes, *John Bull's Island: Immigration and British Society, 1871–1971*, London, 1988.

2   M. Margoliouth, *The History of the Jews of Great Britain*, London, 3 vols, 1851; J. Mills, *The British Jews*, London, 1851.

3   J. Denvir, *The Irish in Britain*, London, 1892.

4   See, for instance, J. E. Handley, *The Irish in Scotland, 1789–1845*, Cork, 1943, and *The Irish in Modern Scotland*, Cork, 1947; J. A. Jackson, *The Irish in Britain*, London, 1963. More recently, the most important studies are: L. H. Lees, *Exiles of Erin: Irish Migrants in Victorian London*, Manchester, 1979; and two volumes edited by Roger Swift and Sheridan Gilley, *The Irish in the Victorian City*, London, 1985, and *The Irish in Britain, 1815–1939*, London, 1985.

5   The best recent study is Peter Fryer, *Staying Power: The History of Black People in Britain*, London, 1984.

6   Lucio Sponza, *Italian Immigrants in Nineteenth Century Britain: Realities and Images*, Leicester, 1988; Terri Colpi, *The Italian Factor: The Italian Community in Great Britain*, Edinburgh, 1991.

7   Rosemary Ashton, *Little Germany: Exile and Asylum in Victorian England*, Oxford, 1986; Panikos Panayi, *The Enemy in our Midst: Germans in Britain during the First World War*, Oxford, 1991.

8   See his *Anti-Semitism in British Society, 1876–1939*, London, 1979; and *A Tolerant Country? Immigrants, Refugees and Minorities in Britain*, London, 1991.

9   The latest book is David Cesarani and Tony Kushner (eds), *The Internment of Aliens in Twentieth Century Britain*, London, 1993.

10   Panikos Panayi (ed.), *Racial Violence in Britain, 1840–1950*, Leicester, 1993.

11   Dirk Hoerder (ed.), *Labor Migration and the Atlantic Economies: The European and North American Working Classes during the Period of Industrialisation*, London, 1985.

12   Stephen Castles with Heather Booth and Tina Wallace, *Here for Good: Western Europe's New Ethnic Minorities*, London, 1984.

13   Oscar Handlin, *The Uprooted: The Epic Story of the Great Migration that Made the American People*, London, 1951.

1

Pre-nineteenth century communities

In order to fully understand the issues of immigration, ethnicity and racism between 1815 and 1945, an awareness of historical traditions of settlement is required. In some cases the pre-nineteenth century background of a community plays a fundamental role in its history after 1800, as patterns of residence develop which remain until the end of the Second World War. This point particularly applies to the Jewish community from its readmission in the 1650s but similar assertions can be made with regard to Germans in the same period. Patterns of migration also play a role, as the example of the movement of merchants from north Germany illustrates, stretching from the tenth to the twentieth centuries. Similarly, hostility towards outgroups did not suddenly appear at the start of the nineteenth century but had a long tradition stretching back hundreds of years.

The prehistory of newcomers to Britain divides into four periods: first, the age of invasions until the eleventh century; second, continental tradesmen, craftsmen and Jews during the high and late Middle Ages; third, religious refugees, economic newcomers and slaves, c. 1500–1650; and, fourth, a significant take-off in a variety of groups from the mid-seventeenth century until 1815.

Although not strictly immigrants, we should mention the early invasions which helped to create Britain. We can begin with the Romans, who, as well as bringing soldiers and invaders from their own kingdom, also imported citizens of states from the areas subject to their rule, including Gauls, Spaniards, Germans and Africans. After the withdrawal of the Romans, at the start of the fifth century, there followed, in the second half of that century and into the sixth, Angles and Saxons who, as invaders, made their way to southern and eastern England and played a role in the shaping of the country for several centuries. The number of Anglo-Saxons may have reached 50,000–100,000, meaning that they made up as much as 10 per cent of the population. After that invasion came the Danes and Norsemen who settled throughout the country.

The most important invaders consisted of the Normans from the eleventh century. They focused upon the south of England, centred upon London, to which the populations of Norman towns moved, but also colonised much of the rest of the country. Furthermore, William the Conqueror imported soldiers from the continent, a policy continued by his successors. The Normans also played a large role in the first significant settlement of the Jews in England, although some seemed to have lived in the country from as early as the eighth century. Even during the eleventh century, only a small number of Jews, mainly from the Rouen community in France, lived in London.

The settlement of people from the continent in Britain changed after the eleventh century, as they never again consisted of large numbers of invaders and the people they brought with them. 'Immigration from now on was a matter of peaceful entry, and had to fit into a more or less orderly society under unified control.'[1] During the years 1200 until 1600 a series of groups made their way to Britain, which we can consider as distinct ethnic minorities.

Firstly, the Jews, whose numbers expanded upon the early base of the twelfth century, and whose position depended fundamentally upon the intensity of the endemic medieval antisemitism at any one time, until it became strong enough to lead to their expulsion in 1290. The end of the eleventh century represents a significant date in the history of the growth of medieval Anglo-Jewry because of a significant influx of refugees from the continent fleeing pogroms at the time of the First Crusade. Subsequently, some Jews moved to England from Spain, Italy and even Russia. Numbers of Jews in medieval England, like the figures for all communities before the mid-nineteenth century censuses, prove difficult to estimate. As many as 5,000 may have lived in England in 1200, 0·25 per cent of the urban population. Other estimates suggest figures varying from 2,500 to 16,500 in 1290.[2]

11

With regard to geographical concentration, Jews initially focused heavily upon London. In fact, no Jewish community seems to have existed outside the capital during the reign of Henry I (1100–35). However, by 1194 Jews resided in twenty locations outside London and by the first half of the thirteenth century provincial settlements included seventeen of the larger towns, amongst them Bristol, Cambridge, Exeter, Gloucester, Lincoln, Oxford and York. In all, over seventy locations may have counted Jewish communities during the eleventh and twelfth centuries.

The best known occupation of Jews in medieval England consisted of moneylending, a trade forbidden to gentiles by religious law. However, they clearly played a role in other occupations. These included clerks and agents living off the moneylenders. Jews also became doctors, and peddlers of cloth, corn and wool, as well as, lower down the social scale, goldsmiths, soldiers, vintners, fishmongers and cheesemongers. The 'great majority' of Jews lived 'either in a state of abject poverty or bordering on that condition',[3] depending heavily on service to their co-religionists. Jewish women, meanwhile, also became involved in moneylending.

A strong Jewish ethnicity, having connections with co-religionists in other European locations, existed in medieval England, fundamentally influenced by the endemic persecution which Jews faced. In the first place this ethnicity manifested itself in the fact that 'Jews naturally tended to live close to each other in most towns, in an area known as "the Jewry"'.[4] Marriages tended to take place, after betrothal, to other Jews. The Jewish communities had their own communal life, allowing, amongst other things, the imposition of internal taxation. Until the end of the thirteenth century most of the important Jewish settlements counted at least one synagogue. Jewish learning also flourished in medieval England, using mostly Hebrew, although English Jews actually spoke Norman French, reflecting their origins.

As mentioned earlier, the situation of medieval Anglo-Jewry fundamentally depended upon the level of antisemitism at any one time. This manifested itself both officially and unofficially. With regard to governmental prejudice, this remained at a low level during the course of the twelfth century but took off in the thirteenth, eventually leading to the expulsion of the Jews. The year 1245 represents an important point because an Act of

12

that time forbade Jews from settling in new locations. Further measures followed as the century progressed, limiting their ability to act as moneylenders until, in 1290, they faced expulsion under Edward I. In addition, local authorities had acted against Jews, most graphically illustrated by their ejection from Leicester in 1231.

The official hostility went with widespread popular antisemitism which manifested itself in two ways in particular: ritual murder accusations and violence. The former revolved around the idea that Jews killed Christian children in order to use their blood either as part of the passover ritual or for medical purposes. The most famous accusations in medieval England occurred in Norwich in 1144 and Lincoln in 1255. Violence against Jews occurred with greater regularity and brutality than racial attacks at any other time in British history. Indeed, for some Christians, their 'first introduction' to a Jew 'was often a riot'.[5] The worst pogroms occurred in 1190 in York, resulting in 150 deaths. However, anti-Jewish riots broke out elsewhere at the same time, including Dunstable, Lynn, Stamford and Bury St Edmunds. In the last of these fifty-seven Jews died. Between 1262 and 1266 further murders of Jews occurred in Worcester, Northampton, Canterbury, Lincoln and Ely.

The history of 'Germans' in medieval England resembles that of Jews. In the first place, they focused upon one particular occupation in the form of trading, representing the English branches of the northern European Hanseatic League. The main settlement, established as the Hanseatic *Kontor* in 1281, lay in London, although German merchants had lived in the capital from the tenth century. Most of the merchants originated from north German towns. By the fourteenth century branches of the Hansa also existed in Ipswich, Yarmouth, Hull, York and Newcastle. The history of German merchants in England also resembles that of Jews in the sense that rising hostility towards them eventually led to their expulsion, although this did not actually happen until 1598, and only lasted for seven years.

Other minority groups also lived in medieval England. From the end of the thirteenth century colonies of Italian merchants, from Genoa and Venice, began to develop on the Thames, while another grew in Southampton. After the expulsion of the Jews, Lombards became especially important in banking. In addition, as with Germans, temporary migrants made their way to England from Italy, including 'artists, writers, musicians, scholars and churchmen'.[6]

French groups in medieval London included merchants from Gascony, who traded mostly in wine. The Irish had begun to make their way to Britain from the twelfth century, many of them working as street vendors and labourers, although others fell into the massive medieval underclasses, leading to the passage of a statute in 1243 to expel Irish beggars. In addition, other groups from farther afield in Europe also lived in medieval London, including Greeks and Spaniards.

From the sixteenth century, although some of the patterns of immigration and the groups concerned remained similar to their medieval predecessors, a series of new minorities began to enter the country. Dealing with the latter, in the first place, religious refugees, fleeing especially from the Counter- Reformation, made their way to England from various countries, especially France, Germany and the Low Countries, although others originated from farther afield. In 1548 Calvinist services took place in Canterbury, and by 1550 foreign congregations existed in London and other parts of southern England. The largest and most important centred on the Austin Friars' church in the capital, which received its charter in 1550, and of which Johannes Lasco, a Polish nobleman, acted as spiritual leader and superintendent. Germans, French, Walloon and Flemish people worshipped separately here in their own language, while the Germans even had a Sunday school. The accession to the throne of the Catholic Queen Mary forced foreign Protestants to leave the country, but they returned when Elizabeth became monarch in 1558.

In fact, a larger influx of religious refugees took place during her reign, consisting of three groups. The first two fled from the suppression of the Dutch Revolt by the Low Countries' Habsburg ruler the Duke of Alva in the late 1560s. They divided into Walloons, who spoke a French dialect and came from the southern Netherlands, or present-day Belgium, and the Flemings or Dutch, who came from farther north. The third group consisted of French Protestants, or Huguenots, who moved to Britain following the massacre of St Bartholemew's Day in 1572, and who represented an early element in a stream that continued into the eighteenth century.

14

Some of the late sixteenth century refugees settled in locations in south-east England outside London. Norwich, Colchester and Sandwich represented three especially important towns. The figures for 'strangers' in these places totalled 3,000 in Norwich in 1569, 431 in Colchester by 1573, and 1,947 'Flemish strangers who emigrated to, or were born in Sandwich'.[7] Other places of settlement in the south-east included Harwich, Dover, Yarmouth and Lynn.

The economic activities of the sixteenth century Protestant refugees revolved around textiles, an activity they and their descendants continued into the 1600s. In both Norwich and Colchester they involved themselves in bay production, while those in Sandwich found employment in a wider range of industries, a situation similar to that in London, where, although clothing and textiles employed most immigrants, others found work in a wide variety of trades, including transport, jewellery and leather.

The Protestant refugees continued to practice their religion. In Norwich, for instance, both the Walloon and the Flemish communities had their own churches, while Colchester had a Flemish minister from 1571. The greatest and most varied religious activity took place in London. The French church there had a membership of over 1,500 from the late 1560s to the 1580s, while the Austin Friars' church, which became Dutch, had 1,850 members in 1583 and still carried out forty-two baptisms as late as 1680.[8]

Despite initially facing a warm welcome from the authorities in many of the areas where they settled, the Protestant refugees subsequently endured hostility. In Sandwich this took the form of local legislation which moved to control, for instance, the economic activities in which the Flemish residents could play a part, although similar measures subsequently came into operation in other locations in south-east England, including London. Popular xenophobia accompanied legislation. In Colchester the newcomers faced classic anti-alien accusations of holding themselves aloof from English society and taking the jobs of Englishmen. Riots against refugees occurred quite regularly, including disturbances in London in 1586, 1593, 1595 and 1599. The most serious attacks took place in Norwich in 1570 in connection with a more general political uprising.

Apart from foreign Protestant refugees, another group which began to appear from the sixteenth century consisted of Black

15

people, most of whom made their way to Britain as slaves. As early as the beginning of the fifteenth century, James IV of Scotland had a series of Africans attached to his court. In England the first five African slaves arrived in 1555. Their numbers grew as the century progressed, but by the 1590s hostility began to arise towards them so that in 1601 Queen Elizabeth authorised the deportation of all 'Blackamoores' from her realm. Although some stayed in the country during the first half of the seventeenth century, they remained few in number.

Gypsies also began to make their way to Britain during the sixteenth century from many parts of Europe but faced much official legislation against them. Furthermore, more established groups also continued to move into Britain including German and Italian travellers, craftsmen, miners, scholars, artists, industrialists and merchants. The Italian church in London had a membership of 150 in 1568. Both German and Italian merchants became victims in the xenophobic riots of 1517 known as 'Evil May Day'.

The Irish also continued to move into Britain, especially in order to escape the 'relentless warfare' in their country. 'Speaking a different language and coming from a less regimented if besieged tribal society', most of the immigrants 'again sought solace in the lower echelons of the host society.'[9] Once again they faced hostility which ranged from that found in serious literature to the passage of another Act to expel Irish vagrants in 1629. Finally, despite the expulsion of 1290, Jews continued to move into England from the fourteenth century until their readmission in the 1650s and 1660s, although their numbers always remained small and they practised their religion secretly. In 1609 those within the country again faced expulsion.

The period from the end of the English Civil War until the early nineteenth century represents a fundamental phase in the history of immigration to Britain, since when the flow of newcomers has remained constant. Some groups represented a growth of previous movements, especially Protestant refugees and Black slaves, while for others this period laid the foundations for the growth of major ethnic communities during the course of the nineteenth century, as the examples of the Germans, Jews and Irish demonstrate.

The French Huguenot refugees at the end of the seventeenth century represent a continuation of the previous streams of such migrants from France in the 1570s. Both before and after the revocation of the Edict of Nantes, which had granted religious toleration, by Louis XIV in 1685, between 150,000 and 180,000 Huguenots left the country, of whom as many as 50,000 may have made their way to England.[10] They originally focused upon London but subsequently moved to other settlements in southern England, from Ipswich to Plymouth. Like their sixteenth century predecessors the Protestant refugees of 100 years later became heavily involved in textiles, especially silk weaving, a particularly important activity in east London. Other trades included watch and clock making, jewellery and even the professions. The Huguenots developed a rich religious life in the areas where they resided, as well as establishing schools. Initially, they faced a positive reaction from British society, manifesting itself particularly in the establishment of funds to assist them upon their arrival. However, 'the popular picture of a uniform welcome for the Huguenots is naive'[11] as they endured hostility both because of their perceived economic threat and cultural distinctiveness, facing identification with the French King Louis XIV, and his foreign policy, from which they had fled.

Another group which took off during the late seventeenth century, and, in this instance, remains significant into the early nineteenth, although not beyond, consists of Black people, who made more of an impact in this period than in any other until the post-1945 years. The reason for the growth of the Black population lay in the development of the slave trade, and the use of African slaves in British colonies in the West Indies. Black people found their way to Britain when brought to the country by returning sugar planters or slave ship captains. Other slaves, Asians and Africans, 'were brought by government officials and army and navy officers returning from service abroad and by captains of ordinary merchant ships'.[12] Other Africans arrived as free sailors, who had served on ships.

Estimates vary as to the number of Black people who lived in Britain at any one time, but the figure generally accepted for the eighteenth century lies between 10,000 and 15,000. The main areas of settlement consisted of London and the other major slave ports of Bristol and Liverpool. For much of the eighteenth century most Black people in Britain had the status of slaves, working as 'servants, stable-boys, grooms, valets or butlers in the houses of titled people and the eminent'. In the late eighteenth century free Blacks in London worked as 'crossing sweepers, sellers of tracts, fruit vendors, entertainers and beggars'.[13] Men made up 'the overwhelming majority of Negroes in England, from the seventeenth to the late eighteenth century'.[14] The slave women acted as maids, while the free ones worked in a variety of occupations, including laundry and sewing work, as well as prostitution.

By the end of the eighteenth century a Black ethnicity had developed in London involving informal meetings in public houses. However, in the early nineteenth century, this ethnicity disappeared owing to the fact that Black people no longer moved to England in large numbers, as well as the lack of Black women, which meant that Black men married Englishwomen, whose children disappeared into white society.

Few groups in British history have become victims of a racism as wide-ranging as that faced by Blacks in eighteenth century Britain. Their status as slaves represented their dehumanised nature, as for much of the century they were essentially property which could be bought and sold, although by the early 1800s slavery had largely disappeared in Britain. However, other forms of racism remained endemic throughout the period. Popular opinion of Blacks, reinforced by attitudes towards Africa, saw them as indolent, 'stupid' and 'promiscuous and strongly sexual',[15] as well as a burden on the poor rates. In fact, the last view resulted in a failed deportation scheme to Sierra Leone in 1787.

Unlike the Black communities, which disappeared early in the nineteenth century, the German, Jewish and Irish ones have a solid continuity from the seventeenth to the twentieth centuries, with the period 1650–1800 playing a fundamental role in their development. Beginning with the Germans, a series of migratory movements took place during this time. A distinctive one occurred in 1709, involving a stream from the Palatinate, due to a combination of political and economic factors, bringing up to 15,000 people to London, most of whom, however, subsequently moved on to the United States. Other Germans also found themselves in England as a result of the Atlantic crossing, which meant that they had to make a stop in the country. The earlier industrialisation of Britain also attracted businessmen and merchants. The latter also proceeded to Britain as a result of the decline of the continental fair, which meant that they wished to make direct contact with their customers. The accession of the House of Hanover to the throne in 1714 acted as a further magnet for Germans.

German settlement in eighteenth century Britain overwhelmingly concentrated upon London, but it encompassed a wide range of social classes and occupations. Apart from the merchants mentioned above, who stood at the top of the social scale, other prominent groups included, lower down, musicians, and sugar bakers in east London who would continue to work in that area into the nineteenth century.

The German community of London developed a sophisticated ethnicity from the 1670s, with the formation of the first exclusively German church in London in that decade. Three more followed by 1700, and by 1810 a further three had come into existence, one of them Catholic. All of these churches lay in the City, Westminster or the East End, although they had already begun to move around with the German population. Both St Mary's Lutheran Church in the Savoy and St George's in Whitechapel had schools attached to them by the beginning of the nineteenth century. Furthermore, by 1815 two of the major German charities of the next 100 years had come into existence, the German Society of Benevolence and the Society of Friends of Foreigners in Distress.

Germans in eighteenth century Britain faced a series of strands of hostility. In the first place, the Hanoverian succession attracted negative attention. The Palatine refugees of 1709, meanwhile, caused a peak of hostility, which resulted in a press campaign and attacks upon them. Germans also fell victim to more general xenophobia which affected all 'foreigners in London with an outlandish look' who 'were liable to be roughly treated, or at least abused, by the mob'.[16]

The most important seventeenth century development in the immigration history of Britain was the readmission of the Jews in the 1650s and 1660s, who would, from that date, form one of the most important streams into the country. In the late seventeenth century many of those who made their way to the country, both Sephardic, from the Iberian Peninsula, and Ashkenazi, from central Europe, consisted of merchants. Until the early eighteenth century, the former, escaping from the Inquisition, made up the majority of the newcomers, but this changed from about the 1730s. The immigrants from central Europe, overwhelmingly poor, entered the country for various reasons, in which the antisemitism which they faced played a significant role, manifesting itself either in 'the welter of discriminatory laws that embittered and impoverished'[17] their lives, or in outbreaks of violence.

The Jewish communities varied in structure. By 1800 the number of Jews in England may have totalled between 20,000 and 30,000. Although centred upon London, during the eighteenth and early nineteenth centuries Jewish settlement spread to encompass numerous other locations, reaching, for instance, Exeter, Plymouth, Leeds, Manchester, Liverpool and Edinburgh. Social composition encompassed all groups from the sub-proletariat to, as we have seen, wealthy merchants. Those at the bottom end of the social scale included paupers and criminals. Slightly above these, some Jews worked as domestic servants. Others became peddlers, both itinerant and stationary, of a variety of goods, including jewellery and clothes. On the highest level, Jews became involved in banking and broking, as well as trade.

Ethnicity developed amongst Jews to a greater extent during the eighteenth century than it did even amongst Germans, although it divided between Sephardim and Ashkenazim, with each branch having its own synagogues and charities. The major London places of worship of the two groups consisted of Bevis Marks in the case of the former and the Great and Hambro Synagogues in the case of the latter, all established in the seventeenth century, followed by the New Synagogue in the 1760s. In addition, independent synagogues had also come into existence within the capital, while provincial cities had also developed their own. By 1820 London had numerous Jewish benevolent organisations, including hospitals and charities.

As at all times in British history antisemitism remained endemic in eighteenth century England. Two particular peaks in this period occurred in the 1750s and at the turn of the century. The first revolved around the passage of the Jewish Naturalisation Act in 1753, which faced repeal because of the hostility towards it, while the second focused upon the perceived problem of the Jewish poor within London.

The Irish community also developed to a considerable extent during the eighteenth century, especially in London, although other locations included Liverpool. Furthermore, significant numbers of Irish worked as temporary summer harvesters outside the capital. The reasons for movement are those which caused people to migrate into the nineteenth century, including population growth and 'changes in the structure and organization of the linen industry'.[18] Occupations remained very much those at the lower end of the social scale, ranging from begging and stealing to street selling and bricklaying. In London the Irish lived in insanitary conditions in some of the worst parts of the capital. By the start of the nineteenth century a series of chapels existed for the worship of the Roman Catholic Irish, especially in London, although Liverpool also had four Catholic missions by this time.

As with antisemitism, hostility towards the Irish remained endemic during the eighteenth century. One strand of this hostility had connections with the potent anti-Catholicism of the period, the main driving force of the Gordon Riots of 1780, when Irish businesses came under attack. The constant violence between the English and Irish working classes during the nineteenth century had its parallels in eighteenth century London, with major recorded incidents occurring in 1736, 1740 and 1763.

In addition to the major communities outlined above, other, smaller groups also made their way to Britain in the late seventeenth and eighteenth centuries. For instance, the first Greek Orthodox church appeared in London in 1677, although it only lasted for five years. However, a Greek presence existed in the capital throughout the eighteenth century. Similarly, Russians also lived in London after 1700 as their country of origin developed ties with Britain. Indians further made their way to Britain either as sailors or as servants brought back by employees of the East India Company. In the 1790s refugees from the French Revolution proceeded to England, although this period also coincided with a rise in xenophobia and the passage of the Aliens Act of 1793 which provided wide powers for the control of foreigners, including the possible deportation of those regarded as undesirable.

By the early nineteenth century we can see that the foundations had been laid for some of the most important communities to develop in the century and a half that followed, notably the Germans, Jews and Irish. Both migration patterns and, more especially, ethnic institutions had developed. In addition, racial ideas and traditions of racism had been formulated. Meanwhile, some of the pre-nineteenth century communities had disappeared, although they left some trace, notably the Protestant refugees of the sixteenth and seventeenth centuries from the Low Countries and France, and the Black groupings. The years after 1800 would result in both the expansion of the existing communities and the development of new ones.

Notes

1 V. G. Kiernan, 'Britons Old and New', in Colin Holmes (ed.), *Immigrants and Minorities in British Society*, London, 1978, p. 25.

2 Paul Hyams, 'The Jewish Minority in Mediaeval England, 1066–1290', *Journal of Jewish Studies*, vol. 25, 1974, p. 271; A. M. Hyamson, *A History of the Jews in England*, London, 1908, p. 107.

3 Hyamson, *History*, p. 108.

4 Hyams, 'Jewish Minority', p. 273.

5 *Ibid.*, p. 277.

6 Terri Colpi, *The Italian Factor: The Italian Community in Great Britain*, Edinburgh, 1991, p. 26.

7 The figures come, respectively, from: C. W. Chitty, 'Aliens in England in the Sixteenth Century', *Race*, vol. 8, 1966, p. 133; Nigel Goose, 'The "Dutch" in Colchester', *Immigrants and Minorities*, vol. 1, 1982, p. 263; Marcel F. Backhouse, 'The Strangers at Work in Sandwich', *Immigrants and Minorities*, vol. 10, 1991, p. 75.

8 David Ormond, *The Dutch in London: The Influence of an Immigrant Community, 1550–1800*, London, 1973, p. 7.

9 Kevin O'Connor, *The Irish in Britain*, Dublin, 1974, p. 13.

10 Mark Greengrass, 'Protestant Exiles and their Assimilation in Early Modern England', *Immigrants and Minorities*, vol. 4, 1985, pp. 67, 71.

11 Robin D. Gwynn, *Huguenot Heritage: The History and Contribution of the Huguenots to Britain*, London, 1985, p. 124.

12 Peter Fryer, *Staying Power: The History of Black People in Britain*, London, 1984, p. 19.

13 Edward Scobie, *Black Britannia: A History of Blacks in Britain*, Chicago, 1972, pp. 22, 24.

14 James Walvin, *Black and White: The Negro and English Society, 1555–1945*, London, 1973, p. 52.

15 *Ibid.*, pp. 163–7.

16 M. Dorothy George, *London Life in the Eighteenth Century*, Harmondsworth, 1966 edition, p. 137.

17 Todd M. Endelman, *Radical Assimilation in English Jewish History, 1656–1945*, Bloomington, Indiana, 1990, p. 34.

18 Brenda Collins, 'Proto-industrialisation and pre-Famine Emigration', *Social History*, vol. 7, 1982, p. 127.

2

Immigration into Britain
1815–1945

The total number of immigrants making their way to Britain in the years 1815–1945 surpassed that of all those who had entered the country since the Norman invasion. During this period a series of permanent, as well as some temporary, large scale groupings settled in England. The first of these consisted of the Irish, of whom as many as a million may have settled in Britain from 1800 to 1900. For much of the nineteenth century, until 1891, Germans formed the second largest grouping in Britain after the Irish, reaching a peak of 53,324 in 1911. However, Russian and Jewish Poles surpassed the Germans after 1891, with over 100,000 entering Britain from the 1880s, although Jewish settlement had taken place throughout the course of the nineteenth century from various parts of central and eastern Europe. One of the most concentrated immigrations of any period in British history took place at the beginning of the First World War, when 240,000 Belgian refugees, escaping the German invasion of their country, made their way to Britain, although nearly all of them had returned home by the end of the war. Little migration took place into Britain for most of the inter-war years, but in the years 1939–45 over 200,000 European refugees made their way to the country, approximately half of them Poles. As well as these major groupings, other, smaller ones also settled in the country throughout the period 1815–1945, notably Italians, French people, Spaniards, Greeks, Indians, Africans and West Indians, perhaps adding an extra 300,000 to the number of people who moved to Britain in the years 1815–1945. We can guess that between 1·5 million and 2 million immigrants settled in the country during these years so that, while Britain may have represented a country of mass emigration, losing 11·4 million people from 1815 to 1930,[1] it also took in significant numbers.

In order to understand the reasons for the numbers of newcomers settling in Britain, we need to take a broad view of the situation, rather than simply focusing upon individual minorities. It is clear that heavy movement into the country took place during a series of periods, while at other times immigration virtually dried up. The former include most of the nineteenth century, but especially the 1840s, 1850s, 1880s and 1890s, while periods of dearth include the 1920s. One of the aims of this chapter will be to explain the reasons for the changes in numbers of immigrants at different times. In addition, it also seeks to establish why different groupings have made their way to Britain on a particular scale.

Countless theories have developed since Ravenstein's at the end of the nineteenth century to explain migration. Political thinkers and political scientists, sociologists, psychologists and historians have all tried to develop explanations for movement. However, none of these has applied to Britain in the nineteenth and early twentieth centuries. Only Robert Miles has come close to developing any sort of theory,[2] while Colin Holmes has avoided doing so, although, importantly, he recognises that 'a range of influences need to be taken into account in any ideal analysis'. Here he includes 'conditions in the country of origin, and in the place of destination, as well as the mechanism by which movement can be achieved'.[3] Wolfgang Köllman and Peter Marschalck, in a study of nineteenth century German emigration to North America have also recognised the complexity of factors involved.[4] Klaus J. Bade, meanwhile, has developed a theory of migration into and out of Germany which asserts that Germany changed from a country of emigration to one of immigration as the economy developed from a poorer agrarian one to a rich industrial one.[5] Marxist-based theories have had the largest impact in academic circles, revolving fundamentally around pull factors in the country of destination, in which the higher wages of industrialised countries attract newcomers from poorer ones, a process in which the state and/or big business play a central role.

The present chapter accepts that Marxist ideas have some elements of truth but cannot apply fully to Britain between 1815 and 1945. Instead, it will move forward with an apparently more traditional approach, but one which tries to provide a more complete explanation for all the movements into Britain over such a long time period. In this model push, pull and enabling factors all contribute. Furthermore, it recognises the existence of underlying, medium term and personal factors, as well as differentiating between politically and economically motivated movements, although the distinction often blurs. The model is by no means perfect but offers a solid guide to fully understanding movement to Britain. The importance of the various factors differs from group to group.

We can begin by dividing these factors into economic and political, recognising that in both cases underlying, medium term and individual determinants played a role. In the case of economic factors we can point to economic development and population growth as underlying ones, short term economic crises as intervening ones, and the influence of chain migration as a personal motivation. With political refugees, we can point to the existence of an autocratic regime, a period of repression and the movement of other members of the same political grouping. Once again, we need to point out that this simply offers a guide to understanding, not a model. We will fully comprehend all movement only at the end of this chapter when we have progressed through push, enabling and pull factors.

Economic push factors

Beginning with economic push factors, the first point we need to recognise is that the overwhelming majority of people who made their way to Britain in the period 1815–1945 originated in Ireland or the European continent. Therefore, in order to understand economic causation, attention must first focus upon the underlying developments in the European economies during the nineteenth and early twentieth centuries, especially within the countries from which the major groups of economic immigrants made their way to Britain: Ireland, Germany, Russia and Italy.

Substantial population growth was a factor common to the above four countries during the course of the nineteenth century and represents an important prerequisite of the mass migration from all of them. In the history of Europe the nineteenth century is an important point in the development of population, changing from a small stable demographic structure which had characterised the early modern period, progressing through sudden growth, caused mainly by a decline in mortality, before a movement to the larger stationary population which characterises twentieth century Europe. The nineteenth century essentially represents a period of readjustment, when sudden population growth created pressure on resources. The increase began in western Europe and moved southwards and eastwards. The Irish population, for instance, grew 'from about 6 million in 1801, to 8 million in 1841', although it subsequently fell,[6] while Germany showed a steady increase from 24,831,000 in 1816 to 64,568,000 by 1910.[7] Similar patterns reveal themselves in Italy and Russia. In the former, the population went from 21,776,824 in 1861 to 34,671,377 in 1911,[8] while in the latter the Jewish population rose from 2,400,000 in 1851 to 5,600,000 in 1910.[9] Nevertheless, population growth in itself does not cause migration; it simply increases its likelihood. Representing the deepest level of causation, it acted as a prerequisite in the nineteenth century because of the pressure it created on resources. Other factors have to exist for demographic change to result in an exodus.

Changes in the economic system of production represents one such factor and various interpretations exist to explain how this plays a role. One idea, which Walter D. Kamphoefner[10] and Brenda Collins[11] have applied to western Germany and parts of Ireland respectively during the first half of the nineteenth century, revolves around the concept of the collapse of proto-industrialisation, whereby labour intensive cottage industries are destroyed under the threat of more cheaply produced British industrial goods, leading to emigration because of the consequent unemployment. Nevertheless, while this explanation may apply to particular parts of Ireland and Germany, it again represents just one push factor, and, in the case of both Germany and Ireland, does not apply to the entire country for the whole course of the nineteenth century, although we should not deny that it provided an early stimulus. We might actually broaden this theme further and suggest that migration inevitably takes place in the early stages of industrialisation because of the deterioration of conditions for those left out. In late nineteenth century Russia, for instance, the economic position of Jews worsened, partly under the impact of early industrial growth.

However, we need to add yet another underlying push factor here in the form of changes on the land which apply to all the major European emigration societies of the nineteenth century. We can begin with Ireland, where several developments before 1850 had an influence upon migratory movements, although they remain fundamentally tied to population growth and its effects. First, land ownership, which inevitably changed under the impact of the rising numbers of people, with a consequent deterioration in living conditions. Land holdings underwent subdivision, which meant 'either division of land among two or more sons whose families would then be reared on a holding which in the previous generation had supported only one family, or else part of a family plot could be sub-let to an under-tenant'.[12] Consequently, just before the Famine, Irish smallholders lived in 'legendary'[13] poverty. We also need to consider the change in the produce farmed in eighteenth and early nineteenth century Ireland, which by the 1840s focused heavily upon the potato so that in 1845 'the potato formed about one third of all tillage output and around 3 million people were dependent exclusively upon it for food',[14] which had serious consequences when this crop failed in the late 1840s.

In Germany, patterns of land ownership, again connected with population growth, also acted as a background factor in emigration. In the south-west of the country, where emigration took off from the eighteenth century and continued apace into the second half of the nineteenth, division of estates amongst all heirs meant that, with rapid population growth, land holdings became too small to sustain a family. In the north-east of the country, the main area of emigration at the end of the nineteenth century, a different pattern emerged whereby the eldest son inherited the estate. However, this had the same effect because, for those who obtained nothing, emigration became almost inevitable, until Germany had industrialised sufficiently to absorb its own surplus population by the 1890s, leading to internal migration to the industrialised parts of the country.

In Russia in the second half of the nineteenth century, the emancipation of the peasants and their consequent movement into urban districts may be viewed as a background land factor in stimulating Jewish emigration in that the new populations of the growing cities competed for resources with the Jewish population already living there. The effects of population growth in Russian

Poland during the second half of the nineteenth century had similar effects.

The classic study of Italian emigration lists numerous agricultural, and even topographical, background factors which led to migration, including the unfair distribution of land, lack of peasant land ownership, low agricultural productivity, and even the incidence of malaria, all of which we need to superimpose upon population pressure.[15] However, for our purposes we also need to focus upon the particular areas from which Italians in nineteenth century Britain originated, as research has pinpointed these to the Como, Parma and Lucca valleys in the north of Italy and the Liri valley north of Rome. An important factor in the northern areas again concerned the break-up of land into small parcels, compelling peasants to attempt to find other ways in which to sustain themselves, which often proved insufficient.

Population growth and agricultural and industrial change represent the underlying economic push factors which we need to consider when attempting to understand emigration from European states. In addition, medium term factors can also operate in some cases, because an examination of movement from Ireland or Germany demonstrates that, while both countries suffered large scale population loss throughout the course of the nineteenth century, particular peaks occurred. In the case of Germany, these took place on at least five occasions and our concern lies particularly with the first two, which took place just after the Napoleonic wars and in the years 1846–54, the second period also representing a significant one in Irish emigration. The importance of both periods lies in the fact that they represent times of severe economic hardship. When distress is put against the background factors already outlined, in which some migration has already taken place, the trickle becomes a flood.

A post-war crisis affected much of Europe immediately after the end of the Napoleonic wars. In Germany, 1816 witnessed 'the worst agricultural catastrophe anybody could remember'[16] and the climax of a series of bad harvests and severe winters which had destroyed the vine crop, affecting south Germany, Switzerland and Alsace. There followed an increase in wheat prices and consequently hunger, resulting in hopelessness and an almost spontaneous stream of families out of south-west Germany, totalling about 25,000 in the years between 1816 and 1819.

The next economic crisis affected emigration in both Germany and Ireland on a much bigger scale and represents the same medium term factor which led to the outbreak of the 1848 revolutions. In Germany, the year 1845 resulted in a below-average crop yield in many parts of the country, and in the following year there followed potato, rye, wheat and fruit failures. During the early 1850s similar agricultural failures took place affecting a wide variety of crops. Inevitably, widespread distress followed these developments, leading to the emigration of 1,360,000 Germans between 1846 and 1858, although enabling factors, discussed below, played a fundamental role in this process.

Although Irish emigration had taken place before the Great Famine of the late 1840s, the events of those years completely changed the numbers moving abroad. Previously, as well as the movements described above, a spurt of emigration had taken place in 1821–3, following another potato crop failure. But the disaster of the late 1840s took place on a massive scale. 'During the period 1845–8 the potato crop failed completely and one million Irish died of disease and starvation.' Between 1849 and 1852 about 200,000 people emigrated, about half of them to Britain.[17] 'Between 1846 and 1854 approximately 1·75 million Irish left the country.'[18] As a result of both deaths and emigration, the population of Ireland fell by about 20 per cent between 1841 and 1851.[19] Those with the lowest and highest rates of pauperism suffered the lowest emigration rates. 'In the former case, people lacked an incentive to leave; in the latter they lacked the means.'[20] Areas affected covered much of the country, moving from the richer provinces of Ulster and Leinster in the north to include poorer districts in the west and south-west. As in the case of Germany, a series of enabling factors, discussed below, assisted the emigration.

Can we detect personal reasons, linked with economic push factors, which caused people to migrate? In the section on pull factors, attention will focus upon chain migration, whereby migrants move to an area where their friends and relatives already live. In this section, our concern essentially lies with whether or not people moved in families. The answer to this depends upon which nationality receives consideration in which period. In the case of Germans, figures indicating a fairly equal proportion of men and women, as well as a significant percentage of children, suggest the movement of family groupings. In the case of Ireland, women outnumbered men as emigrants by the end of the nineteenth century. While a partial explanation of this may lie in an increase in family movement,[21] especially at the time of the Great Famine, another, more recent one suggests that many single women left in order to escape the fact that they could not secure a husband in Ireland without a dowry.[22] In the case of Russian and Polish Jews the movement consisted largely, but not exclusively, of families. The parents of Joe Jacobs, for instance, arrived as individuals, both escaping failed marriages (see Document 1). Italian migration, meanwhile, remained predominantly single male and involved both adults and children. The parents of some of the children employed as street musicians 'sold' them to *padrone*, who would train them and take them to European and North American cities for several years. Clearly, personal motives can cover a wide range, but they need to stand against the background of the underlying economic push factors.

The above discussion has concentrated almost entirely upon the cases of Germany, Ireland, Italy and Russia during the course of the nineteenth century. Do economic push factors operate at other periods and with regard to other countries? In some cases we can give a negative answer, as with those instances where political persecution clearly played the decisive role, such as World War I Belgium or Nazi Germany. In other instances, we can suggest that pull factors played a decisive role, as with labour recruitment from the West Indies in the Second World War. In fact, as we shall see, pull factors played the determining role in most migration from the West Indies, Africa and India in the nineteenth and early twentieth centuries. Other cases prove more difficult, as the discussion below indicates.

Political push factors

Having considered economic push factors, we can now move on to examine political ones. We might ask whether we can apply a three tier level of causation, encompassing underlying, medium term and personal factors. In some cases this seems to contain truth, as with Germany and Russia from 1815 to 1945. In both instances, we speak of an underlying autocratic system from which small numbers of refugees regularly fled, and whose numbers increased dramatically at particular periods such as 1848–50 and 1933–9 in Germany, and during the late Tsarist and early revolutionary period in Russia. However, in other instances, such as Belgium in World War I, the reasons for movement prove spontaneous, as do those for migration from European states in the Second World War, unless we wish to consider both as the consequences of the extension of German autocratic government, which we will do for the purposes of this exercise. We can proceed on a state by state basis, examining Germany, Russia and then other states of origin, which have sent smaller numbers of refugees abroad, such as France and Italy.

The historical development of Germany during the nineteenth and early twentieth centuries involves its progression from an autocracy, in various forms, to its eventual emergence, in 1948, as a liberal democracy. In the intervening period, although short periods of liberal freedom existed, notably 1848–9 and 1919–33, the country also endured periods of repression. If underlying factors play a role, then political emigration should have taken place constantly, but this did not happen, as exiles always fled in reaction to an outburst of repression. However, we can view these periods of extreme intolerance as explosions which could take place only against the underlying background of autocracy. Refugee movements to Britain took place as a consequence of German-centred repression on numerous occasions during the years 1815–1945.

In the nineteenth century, we can identify three groups of refugees. First, those fleeing a clamp-down on the liberal Young Germany movement by the German Confederation during the 1830s, who eventually found themselves in Britain via Switzerland. The most significant nineteenth century grouping moved after the failure of the 1848 revolutions, when as many as 1,150 German refugees may have moved to Britain.[23] A further influx of political newcomers from Germany occurred after the passage of the Anti-Socialist Laws in October 1878, in response to two assassination attempts on the Kaiser. In the case of all three nineteenth century German movements, personal motivations played a role, as we can see from the fact that political groupings transplanted themselves to London.

During the twentieth century more substantial movements made their way to London as a consequence of German repression. The first of these involved perhaps the biggest movement ever over such a short period of time in the form of the 240,000 Belgian refugees who had made their way to Britain by 1918,[24] fleeing from German invading armies, and nearly all of whom returned when the war ended. Hundreds of thousands of people moved to Britain as a result of the savage repression of the Nazis. In the first place we can point to the Jewish refugees who fled the dehumanising official and unofficial antisemitism, which manifested itself, in the case of the former, in legislation depriving Jews of employment and citizenship, as well as encouraging them to emigrate, while the popular hostility culminated in the state-inspired *Kristallnacht* pogrom of 9 November 1938, which resulted in ninety-one deaths. Under such circumstances, almost 400,000 Jews left the Third Reich between 1933 and 1941.[25] During the Second World War a further 100,000 refugees fled to Britain from the European countries invaded by the Nazis, including Norwegians, Danes, Dutch, Belgians and French people, together with German and Austrian Jews who had escaped to these states previously. In addition, by the end of the war 249,000 Poles had made their way to Britain, as a result of both German and Russian attitudes towards their country[26] (see Document 2).

This takes us to the other main source of political refugees in Britain during the nineteenth and twentieth century: Russia. Again, as with Germany, the political system of the country rested upon various forms of autocracy throughout the period 1815–1945, interspersed with bouts of increased reaction, which caused waves of population movements. At least three groups were affected, consisting of Poles, Jews and revolutionaries. Returning to the Poles, as well as those who made their way to Britain in the Second World War others had fled from the partitioned state after the failed revolutionary outbreaks of 1830–1, 1848, 1863–4 and 1905.

The importance of antisemitism in the flight of Russian Jews in the late nineteenth century proves difficult to establish because, as we have seen, economic background factors played an important role in their movement. Contemporary observers had no doubt about the role of Tsarist antisemitic policies, which manifested themselves in a variety of ways, including restrictions upon residence and quotas upon employment in the professions (see Document 3). Most potently, the antisemitism surfaced in severe pogroms on numerous occasions from 1881, especially in that year, following the assassination of Tsar Alexander II. Other serious outbreaks of racial violence occurred in 1903 and 1905. Perhaps we can best explain the role of the potent antisemitism by placing it as an intermediary factor against the background of the economic deterioration in the position of Jews in late nineteenth century Russia.

More purely political exiles also fled from Russia at the start of the twentieth century, more directly as a result of Tsarist repression, including Lenin, who moved to London. After the Russian Revolution over one million refugees fled the country, most moving to France and Germany, with only 15,000 entering Britain.[27]

Political exiles also made their way to Britain from other countries in the period 1815–1945. In all cases they came from states with illiberal constitutions, but always in response to short term crises, with people often moving together with others of a similar political position. Several hundred Italians arrived following the failure of the 1821–2 and 1831 revolutions on the peninsula, while others fled Italy after the failure of the 1848 revolutions,[28] together with French and Hungarians. Further French refugees arrived after the suppression of the Paris Commune in 1871.[29] Several hundred thousand Spaniards fled the Civil War in their country during the 1930s, but only about 4,000, consisting of Basque children, progressed to Britain.[30]

The above examination of both economic and political push factors only offers a partial explanation of immigration to Britain, essentially simply providing the background. In order to understand fully why people entered the country, attention must focus upon the economic and political factors which attracted the groups outlined above to Britain in particular numbers at different times. However, before examining the attractions of Britain, attention must focus upon enabling factors, because a series of fundamental developments took place during the course of the nineteenth century which made mass migration possible in a manner inconceivable at any time before.

Enabling factors

In essence, two major enabling factors affected the mass migrations of the nineteenth century, with a third one applicable to a large number of incidents throughout the period 1815–1945. The first two revolve around the development of transport and the spread of the idea of emigration, whose effects receive attention below, while the third factor refers to 'assisted migration'. It proves difficult with regard to enabling factors to refer to three levels of causation.

Transport played a fundamental role in the development of the mass migrations across the Atlantic during the course of the nineteenth century and also influenced movement into Britain. Two issues concern us here. First, the route across the Irish Sea, bringing Irish people into the country, and, more complicated, the development of the transatlantic route, which brought transmigrants through Britain, many of whom decided to stay. This proved especially important in the case of Germans and east European Jews, as well as the Irish.

With regard to ferries across the Irish Sea, and especially to Liverpool, several changes took place in the first half of the nineteenth century. First came the development of the steamship in the second decade of the century which 'brought a regularity of channel crossings that sail could not because of the dependence on weather conditions'.[31] The steamships also made the crossing more quickly and cheaply, as the routes across the Irish Sea attracted large numbers of steam packet companies as alternatives to the mail ships which had carried passengers as a method of reducing the cost of 'otherwise unrenumerative sailings'.[32] By 1847 steamships were sailing from eleven different Irish ports to Liverpool, while by 1845 'there were, in all, some twenty steamboats running from Glasgow, Ardrossan and Stranraer to Belfast, Newry, Dundalk, Dublin, Cork, Londonderry and Sligo'.[33] Other ships sailed to ports which included Bristol, Liverpool, Whitehaven and Glasgow. Passengers used the Scottish routes throughout the year, but numbers increased when seasonal migrants made their way to Scotland. More importantly, the availability of shipping played an enormous role in the mass influx of the Irish into Britain, and especially Liverpool, during the Great Famine. In the first six months of 1848 alone 111,905 Irish people arrived in Liverpool.[34]

Many of the Irish who made their way to Britain from the time of the Famine hoped subseqently to proceed to the United States. David Fitzpatrick has used the term 'stepwise' to describe this migratory process. 'Impecunious emigrants could walk and beg their way to a sea port, rough it across the Irish Sea, save a few pounds from casual labour in Scotland and northern England, and ultimately invest their savings in a transatlantic passage.'[35]

Returning to German emigrants, we can again point to similar developments to those which affected Ireland. As well as the speeding up of the journey by steamship, railways helped to transport emigrants to the newly improved German ports of departure in the form of Bremen and Hamburg. Significant from our point of view is the fact that many of the routes across the Atlantic involved sailing to an English east coast port, especially Hull or London, but also Hartlepool and Grimsby, and then travelling by train to a point of departure, usually Liverpool. This process proved especially important in the development of the Liverpool German community, although transmigrants also settled in other parts of the country.

The above factor also played a role in the development of east European Jewish communities in nineteenth century Britain. Harold Pollins has written that 'One sometimes gets the impression that the Anglo-Jewish community was built up of those who did not get to America.' Progressing on similar routes to those used by Germans, they travelled by 'train westwards to Liverpool from Hull, alighted at Leeds or Sheffield, or Manchester, and stayed in the Jewish quarter near the railway station'.[36] Bill Williams has made similar assertions, describing east European Jewish settlements which developed in northern cities from the 1840s as 'the local residue of a movement destined chiefly for the United States'.[37]

Just as important an enabling factor as the development of shipping and the route across the Atlantic was the spread of the idea of emigration, which really began to take off in both Germany and Ireland during the 1840s. In both we can accept Marcus Lee Hansen's view that emigration had become a 'craze' which 'represented the cure for all ills, private and public'.[38] Referring to Germany, rather in the way that democratic ideas became so widespread as virtually to become the obsession which led to the 1848 revolutionary outbreak, so, in the same way, emigration offered an alternative. Those who played a role in the spread of the idea included shipping agents and those representing countries wishing to attract immigrants. Within Germany itself emigration societies and newspapers developed.

In Ireland, throughout the course of the nineteenth century, another enabling factor consisted of 'assisted emigration'. This involved financial subsidies to help people to make their way out of Ireland. They originated from the British government, from the colonial administrations in the destinations of the migrants, and from funding by Irish landlords. Nazi Germany in the 1930s also provides an example of assisted emigration, in the sense that the state, at various times, encouraged movement out of the country, while German Jewish bodies assisted in the process.

Economic pull factors

The above account has essentially described the reasons why the major immigrant groups who made their way to Britain actually left their land of birth. We now have to examine what attracted both the major and the minor groups to Britain. We can return to our model of explanation revolving around economic and political considerations and also based upon the three levels of causation: underlying, medium term and personal. We should realise, however, that the various causes remain very closely linked and that the following simply provides a method of dividing up material for the purpose of analysis.

Beginning with economic causation we can focus upon the most important factor which distinguished Britain from the rest of the world for most of the nineteenth century, and especially contrasted it with the countries from which most economic immigrants originated: it was the first industrial country. In that sense, we may wish to compare it with the United States whose industrial growth sucked in tens of millions of newcomers during the nineteenth and early twentieth centuries. However, a more complex picture exists in Britain, because the size of its economy did not allow it to take in such large numbers and because it had its own growing surplus population to absorb, some of which itself made its way to the United States. In this sense, the earlier and more advanced industrialisation of Britain simply acted as a background factor in the case of most of the minorities it attracted, many of whom moved from a less wealthy to a wealthier economy. For instance, one nineteenth century German author pointed to the fact that many of his countrymen had a perception of a 'rich England, where money lies on the street', which attracted newcomers who arrived 'with little money, without references' and 'little knowledge of the English language', who after several days in hotels found a more permanent home, after which they began to look for employment.[39]

However, we might actually point to several groups where the more advanced economy of Britain played a major role, resembling the attractions of the United States. The first of these consists of the Irish, who could move from the abject poverty of their existence in their homeland to opportunities of employment in Lancashire, London, Yorkshire, the north-east, Scotland and elsewhere in Britain. Several scholars have commented upon the importance of Irish immigrants in the British industrialisation process. For instance, J. A. Jackson has written, with regard to Irish immigrants, that 'The existence of a large pool of cheap labour at a time of national expansion abroad proved an essential ingredient to the rapid industrial advance.'[40] More recently, Robert Miles, a historical sociologist of immigrants in Britain, has written that 'Irish labour was a crucial component of capitalist development.' Referring to the west of Scotland, he asserts that 'it is difficult to see how capitalist industrialisation could have occurred at the scale and speed that it did without Irish labour'.[41] However, the most recent, empirically based, study on this subject has asserted that between the 1820s and 1860s 'The Irish immigrants were simply too small to matter much'.[42] Nevertheless, while we can accept this assertion, we can also point out that Irish immigrants did play some role in the industrialsation process, if only as part of a British labour force which encompassed Ireland as part of Britain. In this way the Irish differed from most other immigrant groups before 1945, although the picture is slightly more complex, because, as we shall see, short term booms in demand for labour certainly created a demand for foreign workers on more than one occasion.

Before moving away from the Irish, we should also mention temporary migrants who made their way to various parts of Britain for much of the nineteenth century, mostly as harvesters. Again, as with industrial workers, we can simply speak of the underlying attractions of a larger economy on the British mainland, as well as one, consequently, with more opportunities. Miles, referring to the early nineteenth century, has put the movement into the context of low agricultural productivity on subsistence farms in Ireland compared with a more advanced England where 'an agricultural revolution was well under way, involving the introduction of labour-intensive crops but only limited mechanisation'.[43] But during the second half of the nineteenth century a decrease took place in the number of temporary agricultural migrants from Ireland to Britain. However, when the movement took place upon a large scale, especially during the 1840s, it involved tens of thousands of migrants making their way to various parts of the British Isles. Arthur Redford divided them into three groups, consisting, first, of those who sailed from Munster to Bristol, originating in Kerry and Cork in the south-west of Ireland and making their way 'through all the counties between Gloucester and Middlesex'. Second, migrants from Connaught, who sailed to Liverpool and worked in counties from Lancashire to Lincolnshire. And, third, labourers from the northern part of Ireland, who sailed to Scotland.[44]

The immigration of Black subjects of the British Empire to their 'motherland' during the nineteenth and early twentieth centuries has fundamental connections with the more advanced economic development of Britain. We should immediately recognise the small numbers involved, which suggests a lack of push factors. Main areas of employment included shipping, which employed South Asians, West Indians, Africans and Chinese. Some increase had taken place in the employment of seamen during the Napoleonic wars because of 'a dearth of British seamen impressed into service in the Navy'.[45] Later, in the 1830s, British ships began to employ Chinese sailors, employed in trading on the China coasts. In general, foreign seamen proved cheaper than English ones, in the case of lascars (Asian seamen) 'being paid between one-sixth and one-seventh of the European rate of pay'.[46] Black seamen, meanwhile, found employment as cooks, stewards or 'able seamen'.[47] As we shall see below, their numbers increased during the First World War labour shortage.

The more advanced British education system acted as an attraction to Africans from the mid-nineteenth century, so that, 'in ever increasing numbers, African traders, chiefs, lawyers and doctors sent children to Britain from Sierra Leone and the Gold Coast for higher education, a few also coming from Lagos and the Oil Rivers'.[48] In addition, the number of Indian students increased during the course of the nineteenth and early twentieth centuries, starting from a base of just four in 1845 to reach nearly 2,000 in 1931.[49]

The underlying economic attractions of Britain also served as a pull factor to large scale businesses of all nationalities which made their way to Britain during the course of the nineteenth and early twentieth centuries, particularly those of German, US and Greek origin. Particular factors apply to each grouping at different time periods, although we may point to a greater internationalisation of trade between 1815 and 1945.

An examination of immigration statistics to Britain in the period 1815–1945 demonstrates peaks and troughs, and we should immediately recognise the fact that the level of newcomers has fundamental connections with the short term condition of the British economy. For much of the nineteenth century, with long periods of continuous economic growth, newcomers could enter the country at will. However, against the background of the rising economic threat of the United States and, particularly, Germany during the late nineteenth century, the British state took measures to control the flow of immigration during the Edwardian years. Similarly, against the economic crisis of the inter-war years, Britain introduced extraordinarily tight controls, which meant that, especially during the 1920s, few of the major refugee groups could make their way into the country. As we shall see below, immigration controls served as a fundamental political pull factor throughout the period under consideration.

While periods of economic recession may have resulted in a reduction in the number of immigrants entering Britain, times of growth or, more accurately, periods of short-term labour shortage, resulted in an increased willingness to import foreign labour. We may see the 1840s and 1850s as such a period, but we need to give consideration, in the case of the Irish, to the fact that the British state has never imposed wide-ranging controls upon movement to Britain and to the overwhelming push factor out of Ireland, as well as geographical proximity. However, more Irish would conceivably automatically have made their way to the United States, had the British economy been in a less healthy state.

The First World War represents a more useful illustration of the effects of an economic boom and consequent labour shortage upon the number of people entering Britain, because of the large variety and size of groups who made their way to the country 1914–18. The authority on Belgian refugee relief during the First World War, for instance, has pointed out that 'But for self-interest the British record on Belgian refugees might have been less generous. The shipment of refugees from Holland was essentially part of British economic policy rather than an exercise in philanthropy.'[50] The Black population of Britain also grew during the course of the First World War, especially in the area of shipping and munitions work, the latter also representing a major sector of employment for Belgians. In addition, Blacks also served in the armed forces, as did Indians, although the former did not become involved in front line fighting. In addition, the British government also launched a scheme for the importation of Chinese to work as non-combatant forces on the Western Front, involving 94,700 people.[51]

Similar developments took place against the background of the labour shortage of the Second World War, resulting in a recruitment of West Indian munition workers and service personnel. In addition, the number of Irish workers also increased. Initially, in June 1940, the British government imposed restrictions on travel between Britain and Ireland. However, with the development of a labour shortage in the former and increased unemployment in the latter, the British Ministry of Labour and the Irish Department of Industry and Commerce signed an agreement to facilitate the movement of Irish workers to Britain.

As well as underlying and medium term economic pull factors, we also need to refer to personal ones, by which we mean chain migration, which has played a fundamental role in the development of the major immigrant groups in recent British history. Those for which we have particular evidence include Germans, Italians and Russian Jews. By chain migration we mean the practice of an individual moving to an area of a country of destination where relatives or people from the same village or part of the country of origin live who can provide assistance, often of a financial nature, with the journey. If we begin with Germans, the main evidence of chain migration lies in the fact that, during the nineteenth century, settlements in individual cities tended to have large numbers of people from the same areas of origin. Liverpool, for instance, contained a significant population from Württemberg and Prussia, while London had an over-representation of Hanoverians and people who originated in Hessen (see Document 4).

Several authorities, notably Terri Colpi, Lucio Sponza and Colin Hughes, have commented upon the fact that the Italian communities in Britain during the course of the nineteenth century originated in specific areas and even villages within those areas. The

South Wales Italian community, for instance, originated to a large extent in the town of Bardi, between Parma and Genoa. Italian cafe owners already settled in South Wales would recruit from this town, offering the newcomers 'a fixed contract, with food, clothes, accommodation and the price of a return fare to Italy at the end of a stipulated period of two or three years'.[52] A similar process had operated with regard to the recruitment of Italian children as music players during the course of the nineteenth century. An examination of Italian settlement in Scotland from 1877 to 1939 reveals that the overwelming majority originated in four provinces within the peninsula, while one town in Lucca provided 13·6 per cent of all Italians in Scotland during this period.[53]

Evidence of chain migration also exists with regard to the development of Russian Jewish communities during the course of the nineteenth century. An examination of the proceedings of the Select Committee on Emigration and Immigration, which reported in 1881, has evidence, as it interviewed individual Russian Jews on their motivation for moving to England. The proceedings point to immigrants meeting their friends and relatives immediately after disembarkation and to written communication between already settled Jews and those who had arrived more recently (see Document 5).

Political pull factors

Having examined the economic pull factors which attracted people to England, we can now turn to the political ones which existed during the period 1815 and 1914. We can again divide these into the three tiers of underlying, medium term and personal. One of the most fundamental underlying perceptions of Britain during the nineteenth century focused upon the idea of the country as a cradle of liberty in comparison with the intolerant and unstable regimes which existed in other European states. While Britain was certainly not a liberal utopia, compared with many of the states from which refugees originated in the nineteenth century, it seemed that way. Britain did not undergo any political revolutions during the course of the nineteenth century, which meant that it did not need to repress them and consequently create refugees. We might see many of the states which sent political migrants to Britain as undergoing, in the period 1815–1945, the same process towards liberal democracy which Britain had passed through during the seventeenth century. Some finally arrived at that situation at the end of World War II, notably Germany, while the Soviet Union did not. The process of arriving at that situation involved serious political upheaval, repression and then progression again.

A series of historians have examined the attractions of Britain to European refugees. Rosemary Ashton, for instance, in her study of German exiles from the 1848 revolutions has listed what she describes as 'the vaunted freedoms enjoyed by Britons and denied to Germans in their own country', which included 'the freedom to set foot in the country of their choice and stay there without fear of expulsion' and 'freedom of speech, of the press, and of association'.[54] Bernard Porter, meanwhile, has pointed to the fact that during most of the nineteenth century refugees moved to Britain at will, often to continue their campaigning 'in an environment which was more tranquil, and more safe'. Furthermore, he points out that individuals of any political persuasion, from communists to autocrats, could move into the country.[55]

Some of the above underlying factors apply to both the nineteenth and early twentieth centuries. However, one fundamental difference concerns the ability to enter the country. The history of British immigration policy from the mid-nineteenth century is that of a move from an open door, allowing anyone to enter the country from any place of origin, to a continual tightening of the restrictions upon who could move into Britain. Immigration control represents a concrete medium term political pull factor which has fundamentally affected the volume of both political and economic immigration into Britain and we can briefly examine the development of British immigration laws and their effects during the years 1815–1945.

As Porter has pointed out, 'from 1826 until 1848, and again from 1850 to 1905, there was nothing on the statute book to enable the executive to prevent aliens from coming and staying in Britain as they liked . . . This freedom of entry applied to all foreigners, whether refugees or not, and for whatever reason they desired entry.'[56] The Aliens Act of 1905 represents the first nail in the coffin of free entry to Britain. It represented a 'watershed for aliens' entry', because it had breached the 'liberal tradition of most of the nineteenth century'.[57] Although its provisions remained quite limited, its importance lies both in its symbolism and in the fact that it put off newcomers from making their way to Britain.

The outbreak of the First World War resulted in the passage of the Aliens Restriction Act, strictly controlling the entry of enemy aliens, and less forcefully dealing with other aliens. Significantly, it did not prevent the entry of Belgian refugees, owing to the labour shortage, demonstrating that all immigration legislation remains selective in the groups it aims to keep out. The Aliens Act of 1919, passed in the anti-alien hysteria of the immediate post-war years, represented another important landmark, giving the Home Secretary power to pass Orders in Council as he wished in order to control any aspect of immigration. The Order of 1920 is the most important, requiring all alien immigrants to obtain work permits, and forbidding anyone who could not support themselves from entering the country. This measure helps to explain the small number of refugees who entered Britain in the inter-war years.

However, the situation changed in the 1930s, especially with regard to Jewish refugees, whose numbers increased as the Second World War approached, owing to a change of British government policy. Initially, the government reacted with indifference, insisting that all newcomers should have the ability to support themselves financially. From 1933 until November 1938 only 11,000 refugees entered Britain, but from that time, when Nazi antisemitism became particularly brutal, as demonstrated by the *Kristallnacht* pogrom, until the outbreak of the Second World War a further 55,000 followed. Earlier in 1938, at the international conference to deal with the refugees from Nazism at Evian, the Home Office had declared that it would adopt a more liberal policy towards admission 'on the grounds of humanity'.[58] Older interpretations of British policy towards Jewish refugees during the 1930s see it in a positive light. A. J. Sherman's 1973 study asserts that the British government acted in a 'comparatively compassionate, even generous' manner, if viewed against the background of the attitudes of other states.[59] However, more recent revisionist interpretations, put forward especially by Tony Kushner and Louise London, question the generosity of British government policy. The former has pointed to the fact that 20,000 of the newcomers entered the country as domestic servants, while Louise London has asserted that the figures increased substantially just before the outbreak of the Second World War because British policy-makers assumed that the newcomers would simply pass through the country.[60]

As well as the underlying liberal traditions of Britain and medium term government policy as political pull factors, we might also point to the fact that refugees have often received an enthusiastic reception from committees established to assist them, which we can almost describe as short term political pull factors. For instance, the late nineteenth century east European Jewish newcomers obtained some assistance from Anglo-Jewish organisations, including the Poor Jews' Temporary Shelter and the Board of Deputies. However, historians have questioned just how welcoming organisations such as these really were, pointing to the fact that the primary concern of the established Jewish community within Britain was to protect its own position rather than assist the entry into the country of its poorer co-religionists.

The Belgian refugees of the First World War would appear to have received a more altruistic welcome from British society. As late as February 1916, twenty-six charities existed for their relief, the most important of which consisted of the War Refugees, Committee, which worked closely with the Local Government Board. However, we need to place the enthusiasm of the reception for the refugees against the background of the First World War and the fact that they operated as a positive symbol in the fight against Germany. In addition, the early positive reaction faded as we can see from the fact that receipts for the War Refugees Committee declined from £53,000 in 1914 to just £4,420 during the last eighteen months of the war.[61]

Government policy towards the entry of refugees during the 1930s was partly eased by the fact that significant numbers of organisations existed to assist them financially. For instance, the 3,899 Basque children who made their way to Britain following General Franco's bombardment of their homes in 1937 received support from the privately funded Basque Children's Committee of the National Joint Committee for Spanish Relief. The Roman Catholic Church and the Salvation Army also assisted them. Initially, they lived in camps (see Document 6).

Jewish refugees from Nazism received help from a wide variety of organisations, both Jewish and non-Jewish. The former included the Jewish Refugees' Committee, which came into existence in

May 1933, and the Central British Fund for German Jewry, which raised £3 million between 1933 and 1940. Christian organisations included the Society of Friends' German Emergency Committee, the International Hebrew Christian Alliance, the Church of England Committee for 'non-Aryan' Christians and the Catholic Committee for Refugees. The non-denominational International Student Service and the Academic Assistance Council helped specific groups of exiles. The Movement for the Care of Children from Germany transported 9,354 children between 1938 and the outbreak of war. They initially went to camps on the east and south-east coasts but by December 1939 about 6,000 had found a place with families, although many had unhappy experiences (see Document 7). The refugees also aroused hostility in the press and amongst professions which viewed them as an employment threat.

Conclusion

Clearly, the reasons for the entry of millions of people into Britain during the years 1815–1945 are extremely complicated, revolving around a complex of economic, political, short term, underlying and personal push and pull factors. The immigration of any individual minority involves a set of factors peculiar to itself. In some cases, such as the mid-nineteenth century Irish, push factors played an overwhelming role, as the famine literally forced people off the land. However, the geographical proximity of Britain and the open door policy towards immigration played a fundamental role in attracting the Irish. In a few cases, such as colonial workers recruited during the two World Wars, pull factors play a fundamental role. However, Britain before 1945 differs from the United States in the nineteenth century, or western Europe since the war, in the sense that no large scale recruitment of labour from less developed countries took place under the influence of government and big business, because of the smaller scale of the British economy, and the availability of surplus labour within the country during a period of significant population growth. For nearly every minority moving to Britain before 1945 a combination of factors played a role.

As we have seen, the entry of immigrants into Britain between 1815 and 1945 did not take place steadily, but occurred in waves.

The periods of relatively low immigration occurred in 1815–45, 1860–80, 1905–14 and 1915–38. The reasons for the variations are complex. The health of the British economy played an important role, because in periods of slump the government imposed stricter legislative controls, while at times of labour shortage it loosened its controls upon entry. We might also point to a move away from the classic British liberalism of the nineteenth century as state control in a variety of aspects of life increased. Furthermore the growth of national and racial consciousness also played a role from the late nineteenth century, as antisemitism began to flourish. The state response plays a central role in controlling the flow of immigration, under the influence of the above factors.

Notes

1 Dudley Baines, *Emigration from Europe 1815–1930*, London, 1991, p. 9.

2 Robert Miles, 'Migration to Britain: The Significance of a Historical Approach', *International Migration*, vol. 29, 1991, pp. 527–43.

3 Colin Holmes, *John Bull's Island: Immigration and British Society, 1871–1971*, London, 1988, p. 278.

4 Wolfgang Köllman and Peter Marschalck, 'German Emigration to the United States', *Perspectives in American History*, vol. 7, 1973, pp. 497–554.

5 Klaus J. Bade, *Vom Auswanderungsland zum Einwanderungsland? Deutschland 1880–1980*, Berlin, 1980.

6 Brenda Collins, 'The Origins of Irish Immigration to Scotland in the Nineteenth and Twentieth Centuries', in T. M. Devine (ed.), *Irish Immigrants and Scottish Cities in the Nineteenth and Twentieth Centuries*, Edinburgh, 1991, p. 2.

7 John E. Knodel, *The Decline of Fertility in Germany, 1871–1939*, Princeton, 1974, p. 32.

8 Luigi Di Comite, 'Aspects of Italian Emigration, 1881–1915', in Ira D. Glazier and Luigi De Roza (eds), *Migration across Time and Nations: Population Mobility in Historical Context*, London, 1986, p. 150.

9 Salo W. Baron, *The Russian Jew Under Tsars and Soviets*, London, 1976, p. 64.

10 Walter D. Kamphoefner, 'At the Crossroads of Economic Development: Background Factors Affecting Emigration from Nineteenth Century Germany', in Glazier and De Roza, *Migration across Time*, pp. 174–201.

11 Brenda Collins, 'Proto-industrialisation and Pre-Famine Emigration', *Social History*, vol. 7, 1982, pp. 127–46.

12 Collins, 'Origins of Irish Emigration', pp. 2–3.

13 Cormac O Grada, *The Great Irish Famine*, London, 1989, p. 30.

14 Collins, 'Origins of Irish Emigration', p. 3.

15 Robert F. Foerster, *The Italian Emigration of our Times*, Cambridge, Massachusetts, 1919, pp. 53–86.

16 Mack Walker, *Germany and the Emigration, 1816–1885*, Cambridge, Massachusetts, 1964, p. 4.

17 Kevin O'Connor, *The Irish in Britain*, Dublin, 1974, p. 20.

18 Lynn Hollen Lees, *Exiles of Erin: Irish Immigrants in Victorian London*, Manchester, 1979, p. 39.

19 Collins, 'Origins of Irish Emigration', p. 8.

20 Lees, *Exiles of Erin*, p. 39.

21 *Ibid.*, p. 49.

22 Pauline Jackson, 'Women in 19th Century Irish Emigration', *International Migration Review*, vol. 18, 1984, pp. 1004–20.

23 PRO, MEPO 43.

24 Holmes, *John Bull's Island*, p. 87.

25 Panikos Panayi, 'Refugees in Twentieth Century Britain: A Brief History', in Vaughan Robinson (ed.), *The International Refugee Crisis: British and Canadian Responses*, London, 1993, p. 101.

26 S. Patterson, 'The Poles: An Exile Community in Britain', in J. L. Watson (ed.), *Between Two Cultures: Immigrants and Minorities in Britain*, Oxford, 1977.

27 Panayi, 'Refugees in Twentieth Century Britain', p. 100.

28 Margaret C. Wicks, *The Italian Exiles in London, 1816–1848*, New York, 1968 edition.

29 Holmes, *John Bull's Island*, p. 35.

30 Panayi, 'Refugees in Twentieth Century Britain', p. 101.

31 Frank Neal, 'Liverpool, the Irish Steamship Companies and the Famine Irish', *Immigrants and Minorities*, vol. 5, 1986, p. 30.

32 H. S. Irvine, 'Some Aspects of Passenger Traffic between Britain and Ireland, 1820–50', *Journal of Transport History*, vol. 4, 1960, p. 225.

33 J. E. Handley, *The Irish in Scotland, 1798–1845*, Cork, 1943, p. 31.

34 Neal, 'Liverpool', p. 34.

35 David Fitzpatrick, *Irish Emigration, 1801–1921*, Dublin, 1984, p. 23.

36 Harold Pollins, *Hopeful Travellers: Jewish Migrants and Settlers in Nineteenth Century Britain*, London, second impression, 1991, p. 25.

37 Bill Williams, *The Making of Manchester Jewry, 1740–1875*, Manchester, 1985 reprint, p. 176.

38 Marcus Lee Hansen, *The Atlantic Emigration, 1607–1860*, New York, 1961 edition, p. 288.

39 Heinrich Dorgeel, *Die Deutsche Colonie in London*, London, 1881, pp. 17, 19–21.

40 J. A. Jackson, *The Irish in Britain*, London, 1963, p. 82.

41 Robert Miles, *Racism and Migrant Labour*, London, 1982, p. 123.

42 Jeffrey Williamson, 'The Impact of the Irish on British Labour Markets during the Industrial Revolution', in Roger Swift and Sheridan Gilley (eds), *The Irish in Britain, 1815–1939*, London, 1989, p. 160.

43 Miles, *Racism and Migrant Labour*, p. 126.

44 Arthur Redford, *Labour Migration in England, 1800–1880*, Manchester, 1964 edition, pp. 145–7.

45 Douglas Jones, 'The Chinese in Britain: Origins and Development of a Community', *New Community*, vol. 11, 1979, p. 397.

46 Rozina Visram, *Ayahs, Lascars and Princes: The Story of Indians in Britain, 1700–1947*, London, 1986, p. 34.

47 T. Lane, *Liverpool: Gateway of Empire*, London, 1987, p. 115.

48 Hans Werner Debrunner, *Presence and Prestige; Africans in Europe*, Basel, 1979, p. 368.

49 Visram, *Ayahs, Lascars and Princes*, p. 178.

50 Peter Cahalan, *Belgian Refugee Relief in England during the Great War*, New York, 1982.

51 Michael Summerskill, *China on the Western Front: Britain's Chinese Workforce in the First World War*, London, 1962, p. 195.

52 Colin Hughes, *Lime, Lemon and Sarsaparilla: The Italian Community in South Wales, 1881–1945*, Bridgend, 1991, p. 47.

53 Andrew Wilkins, 'Origins and Destinations of Early Italo-Scots', *Association of Teachers of Italian Journal*, no. 29, 1979, pp. 57–8.

54 Rosemary Ashton, *Little Germany: Exile and Asylum in Victorian England*, Oxford, 1986, pp. 38, 44.

55 Bernard Porter, *The Refugee Question in Mid-Victorian Politics*, Cambridge, 1979, pp. 1, 2, 3.

56 *Ibid.*, p. 3.

57 Vaughan Bevan, *The Development of Britsh Immigration Law*, London, 1986, pp. 70–1.

58 Louise London, 'Jewish Refugees, Anglo-Jewry and British Government Policy, 1930–1940', in David Cesarani (ed.), *The Making of Modern Anglo-Jewry*, Oxford, 1990, pp. 178, 180.

59 A. J. Sherman, *Britain and Refugees from the Third Reich, 1933–39*, London, 1973, p. 267.

60 See the contributions of Tony Kushner and Louise London to Werner E. Mosse *et al.* (eds), *Second Chance: Two Centuries of German-speaking Jews in the United Kingdom*, Tübingen, 1991.

61 Cahalan, *Belgium Refugee Relief, passim*.

3

The structure of minority groups

Having established the reasons why immigrants made their way to Britain in such large numbers during the nineteenth and early twentieth centuries, we now need to examine their structure, an issue which covers a variety of themes. First, the size of minorities, which varied from, in some cases, a few hundred to, in the case of the nineteenth century Irish, more than half a million. Geographical concentration tended to focus upon London, and particular areas within the capital, for most groupings, although, as we shall see, there were exceptions to this rule. The third theme to be tackled is age and gender, which vary according to the community examined. Many, such as the Chinese and Italians, consisted of young males for much of the period under consideration, while others, notably the Irish, developed a more even age and sex structure during the course of the nineteenth century.

The most important theme covered by this chapter is the economic activities of immigrants in Britain during our period, which indicates the existence of a class structure, further examined in the next chapter, among some of the larger groups. While the majority of immigrants in Britain from 1815 to 1945 may have consisted of those lower down the social scale, we would be wrong to view this as the whole picture. The German, Jewish and Irish communities all reveal a complex class structure, with individuals ranging from the sub-proletariat to the upper bourgeoisie. This class structure directly parallels, yet remains distinct from, English society. Whether or not newcomers of a particular group originated from a capitalist society, once they entered Britain they had to fall in with its social structure.

The size of communities

As mentioned previously, any attempt to measure the numbers within individual minorities before the mid-nineteenth century censuses proves hazardous. Even after this period, we cannot speak with firm confidence about some groupings, notably Jews and Gypsies. However, in some cases, where the minorities consisted mainly of first generation immigrants, measurement proves possible, with a considerable degree of accuracy from the mid-nineteenth century. Table 1 can act as our starting point to this chapter, demonstrating the size of the easily measurable communities in the census years of 1861, 1901 and 1931, the first and last dates representing the earliest and latest dates for which full information exists within our period. For Scotland, figures for foreign communities did not exist in 1861, which explains the fact that only 1901 and 1931 are covered. The information is very basic, simply indicating the number of first-generation immigrants.

The data in Tables 1 and 2 merit considerable analysis and elaboration. The most striking fact is the size of the Irish community, which, in virtually all cases, outnumbers all other groups put together. We also have information about the Irish before 1861, which shows that the number of Irish immigrants in Britain totalled over 400,000 as early as 1841 and had risen to more than 700,000 by 1851, with a peak of 806,000 in 1861.[1] J. A. Jackson has drawn up a table to demonstrate the proportion of Irish to native born in England and Wales and also in Scotland. In the former, the peak year was 1861, where 3 per cent of the population were of Irish birth, while in Scotland in 1851, 7·2 per cent of the population in 1851 had been born in Ireland.[2]

Other striking facts about Table 1 include the consistently large size of the German and French communities, and the growth of the Italian, French and Russian and Polish groupings. The last two of these need further examination, as the explanation for their growth lies essentially in the immigration of Jews in the late nineteenth century, which resulted in important changes in the structure of Anglo-Jewry, as discussed below. However, we should recognise that the number of Jews in England cannot be measured by census statistics, as they do not reveal religious affiliation, which means that practising Jews born in England remain left out. Both contemporary writers and historians have attempted to estimate the size of the Jewish communities in Britain during the nineteenth and twentieth centuries, using various methods such as death rates and attendance at synagogues. In 1830 the number of Jews in Britain may have totalled between 25,000 and 30,000, a figure which probably rose to about 40,000 twenty years later. V. D. Lipman estimates that the number of Jews had reached 60,000 in 1881 and that just after the turn of the century there were about 150,000 Jews resident in Britain, though a contemporary article put the figure at almost a quarter of a million. At the outbreak of the Second World War, with the increase brought about by refugees from Nazism, the Jewish population had reached 370,000.[3]

Tables 1 and 2 have further gaps, in the sense that they do not reveal figures for other groups about which we have information, especially Gypsies and Black and Asian immigrants. With regard to the first of these, David Mayall has measured their size during the nineteenth century by referring to the census figures for people 'found dwelling in barns, sheds, tents, caravans and the open air'. This shows an increase from 20,348 in 1841 to 30,642 in 1911,

Table 1   *Foreign born population of England and Wales, 1861, 1901, 1931*

Birthplace	1861	1901	1931
Ireland	601,634	426,565	381,089
France	12,989	20,797	29,175
Greece	574	997	2,187
Italy	4,489	9,909	20,023
Germany	28,644	50,599	28,048
Russia	1,633	23,626	36,133
Poland	3,616	21,448	43,912
China	146	767	5,793
United States	7,686	19,740	37,420
Total immigrants	685,724	619,678	688,839

Sources: *Census of England and Wales for the Year 1861, Population Tables*, vol. 2, London, 1863, pp. lxxiii, lxxv; *Census of England and Wales, 1901, Summary Tables, Area, Houses and Population*, London, 1903, pp. 258, 260; *Census of England and Wales 1931: General Tables*, London, 1935, p. 221.

Immigration, ethnicity and racism

Table 2   *Foreign born population of Scotland, 1901, 1931*

Birthplace	1901	1931
Ireland	205,564	124,296
France	590	900
Greece	46	71
Italy	4,051	5,280
Germany	3,232	1,154
Russia	7,184	2,806
Poland	3,189	971
China	38	760
United States	690	7,172
Total immigrants	228,191	154,412

Sources: Eleventh Decennial Census of the Population of Scotland, vol. 1, Glasgow, 1902, p. 316, vol. 2, Glasgow, 1903, p. 338; Census of Scotland, 1931: Report of the Fourteenth Census of Scotland, vol. 2, Edinburgh, 1993, p. 112.

although the number had decreased to a low of 10,383 in 1871.[4] Tables 1 and 2 demonstrate the size of Chinese communities but not Black and South Asian ones, which also remained equally small for much of the period 1815–1945. In 1861 only 321 Africans lived in England and Wales, a figure which had increased to 29,036 by 1931, although only 5,232 of these were born outside South Africa, and were presumably not White. Even more confusing is the figure for people born in the Indian Empire in the 1931 census, which stands at 86,963, but we can only assume that the vast majority of these consisted of White Anglo-Indians. Other significant minorities worth mentioning include the 240,000 Belgians who made their way to Britain during the First World War and the Poles who entered the country at the end of the Second World War. Furthermore, as many as 7,000 Lithuanians may have resided in Scotland at the beginning of the twentieth century.[5] In addition, numerous other minorities have been present in Britain during the period 1815–1945, but have left little trace.

Geographical distribution

Settlement patterns on a local level receive more attention in the next chapter on ethnicity. However, at this stage we can provide an introduction to the geographical distribution of some of the best-documented groups in Britain between 1815 and 1945. Two minorities, consisting of the Irish and Jews, become virtually ubiquitous for a section of our period, while the Germans also resided in a large number of locations for much of the nineteenth century. Smaller groupings, as previously mentioned, usually have a concentration in London, although they may also have lived elsewhere.

If we begin with the Irish, we can once again reiterate the point about their widespread settlement throughout Britain, although they certainly concentrated in some areas more than others, especially London, Lancashire and Scotland. 'London had the largest Irish-born population in 1841, some 74,000 or 3·9 per cent of its inhabitants. By 1851 the Irish-born had risen to 108,548, or 4·6 per cent of the total',[6] although after that time it declined steadily. In 1851, however, the Irish had 'moved into every Registrar General's district of the metropolis'.[7] In St Giles in the Fields, St Olave in Southwark and Whitechapel they made up more than 10 per cent of the population. By 1881 the number of Irish living in London had decreased by a third and some movement had taken place out of the above inner city areas to the West End and south of London, although in the 1890s John Denvir's contemporary account of the Irish in Britain identified his countrymen still living throughout the capital (see Document 8).

The surveys of both Denvir and other commentators on the Irish in nineteenth century Britain also point to the heavy concentration of the Irish in Lancashire, closely connected with the geographical proximity of that part of England to Ireland and to the opportunities of employment offered by industrialisation. Liverpool and Manchester contained the greatest concentrations. In the former, the Irish made up 17·3 per cent of the population in 1841, a figure which had declined to 12·6 per cent in 1891, while in the latter the percentage fell from 11·06 in 1841 to 4·6 in 1891. In Liverpool the poor Irish immigrants lived in overcrowded inner city areas, within some of which they formed more than 40 per cent of the population.[8] Both Liverpool and Manchester had contained significant numbers of Irish immigrants before the famine. The latter may have contained 30,000 Irish Catholics in 1832, while the 1841 census put the figure at 30,034.[9] The Irish area of settlement in Manchester received attention from several commentators in the first half of the nineteenth century (see Document 9). Irish settlements also existed in other locations within Lancashire, including Blackpool, Lancaster, Chorley and Preston.

As we have seen, the Irish formed a particularly significant minority in Scotland, especially concentrated in the west of the country. In 1841 the Scottish cities with the highest proportion of Irish immigrants consisted of Lanark, Renfrew, Dumbarton and Wigtown, while Glasgow contained the largest proportion of Irish after Liverpool amongst the major British cities. Other significant Irish locations of settlement in Scotland included Edinburgh, Dundee and Paisley, although they were spread through much of the country, especially in the form of agricultural labourers and navvies.

These two occupational groups also lived throughout northern England in the early part of the nineteenth century. More significant areas of settlement also developed. For instance, in west Cumberland Protestant and Catholic Irish became involved in iron ore production in the second half of the nineteenth century. Bradford's textile industries attracted the Irish in the mid-nineteenth century, where they made up 6·2 per cent of the population in 1871, although the proportion declined during the course of time.[10] In Leeds, where the Irish lived in the east end of the city, they formed over 7 per cent of the population in 1851 and 1861, employed in a variety of trades and residing in poor quality housing.[11] The main occupation of the Irish in York was farming. In the north-east, Irish immigrants settled in Newcastle, Sunderland, South Shields and Gateshead. Elsewhere, we can mention Irish concentrations in the Midlands, especially Birmingham (see Document 10), and South Wales, particularly Cardiff.

As already mentioned, like the Irish, Jews in Britain during the nineteenth and twentieth centuries also lived throughout the country, although a heavier concentration focused upon London, while the other areas of settlement were similar though not identical. Beginning with the capital, about two-thirds of British Jews lived there in the mid-nineteenth century. Alderman estimates that by 1900 about 135,000 Jews resided in London, a figure which had moved to nearer 200,000 by 1929, so that Jews made up just over 4 per cent of the population.[12]

Within the capital, a series of Jewish areas of settlement

developed during the period under consideration. In 1851 about two-thirds of London Jews still lived in the City and its immediate vicinity in the East End. The latter area became the main focus for the east European immigrants of the late nineteenth century, so that in 1911 43,925 out of the 63,105 Russians recorded in the census of that year lived in the East End borough of Stepney.[13] In 1889 east London contained 90 per cent of London's Jews. However, by the early 1930s the situation had changed so that east London housed just 60 per cent of the capital's Jews. By this time movement had taken place out of the inner East End farther north and east to locations such as Hackney and Stoke Newington, and Jewish settlement had 'penetrated into almost every London borough',[14] with settlements, in, amongst other places, Palmers Green in the north, Chingford in the east, and Golders Green, Hendon and Finchley in the north-west, a part of London which attracted many of the refugees from Nazism.

Outside London, Jews had begun to reside in a large number of locations as early as the start of the nineteenth century, so that Cecil Roth's *Rise of Provincial Jewry*, which deals with the period 1740–1840, examines over forty towns inhabited by Jews, 'mainly in county towns, seaports and resort towns'.[15] Some of these disappeared in the first half of the nineteenth century to be replaced by new ones in recently industrialised areas in South Wales, the Midlands and the north-east. The route of transmigrants through England also led to the development of communities in towns through which they passed, including Hull, Newcastle, Hartlepool and Middlesbrough. During the inter-war years, Jews followed the population movements of native society, meaning movement to seaside resorts and out of areas suffering especially badly from the depression.

Several provincial cities developed particularly important Jewish communities during the period 1815–1945. In Manchester, for instance, Jewish settlement had begun in significant numbers in the late nineteenth and early twentieth centuries, to reach 10,000 in 1875 and 30,000 by 1914.[16] Leeds Jewry, meanwhile, had reached about 20,000 by 1905.[17] In Glasgow the Jewish population grew from a 'small provincial community of some 2,000 souls in 1891' to 'become a major centre within a decade with over 6,000 Jews' concentrated mainly in the Gorbals district.[18] A further small increase occurred as a result of the influx of refugees from Nazism during the 1930s. In all the major Jewish provincial communities movement took place out of the original poor areas of settlement into more suburban ones.

If we turn to the German community in Britain, we see that its focus remained primarily in London, where about half the German population lived throughout the Victorian and Edwardian years, concentrating in particular areas within the capital. First, a poor community in the East End, out of which some movement took place at the end of the nineteenth century. By the Edwardian years an important settlement had also taken root in St Pancras, again primarily working class. The main middle class area lay in south-west London, concentrated upon Sydenham. However, by the outbreak of the First World War, Germans lived throughout the capital. Outside London, only miniscule German communities developed, never counting more than 3,000 souls, although this did not prevent a large number of them from supporting churches and other ethnic bodies. The main provincial German communities were in Liverpool, Manchester and Bradford, as well as Hull and Leeds.

With regard to Italians, the refugees of the early nineteenth century focused upon London. Similarly, Lucio Sponza has demonstrated that throughout the period 1861–1911 between 45 and 57 per cent of Italians lived in the capital, a situation which continued into the early twentieth century, as demonstrated by Terri Colpi. Although spread throughout London, a particular concentration developed in Clerkenwell (see Document 11). In contrast to other minorities, a significant percentage of Italians moved to Scotland, so that in 1911 4,594 lived there, while 20,389 resided in England and Wales. By far the major concentration lay in Glasgow, at 1,461 in 1901, followed by Edinburgh with 463. Glasgow's Italian population rose higher to 6,092 in 1927.[19] Other concentrations of Italians existed in Liverpool, the Ancoats area of Manchester, and the South Wales valleys, where numerous Italian cafes, concentrated in particular areas, had developed by the start of the twentieth century, with Cardiff representing a particular focus.

Most of the other European groupings who settled in Britain from 1815 to 1945 had significant concentrations in London. The French community, for instance, had a quarter in Leicester Square during the late nineteenth century, which remained in existence into the

Edwardian period, although by then the French lived 'in almost every London district, and some of the most influential French business men, having their offices in the City, reside in Croydon, which rejoices in quite a colony of Frenchmen'.[20] The Swiss community had focuses upon London and Manchester from the mid-nineteenth century, while consulates also existed in Liverpool, Hull and Glasgow in 1920. By the start of the twentieth century, Greek communities had developed in London, Cardiff, Manchester and Liverpool, originating in the settlement of merchants from the Greek islands. By the 1930s a Greek Cypriot community had developed in the Soho area of London, where most of the immigrants found employment in the hotel and catering trade. Earlier, in the 1820s, a Spanish colony had developed in Somers Town in London, consisting of 'victims of political change in their country', many of them 'professional men or soldiers'.[21] Russian political exiles in the late nineteenth and early twentieth centuries settled in the East End of London. Finally, amongst European groupings, Belgian refugees found accommodation throughout the country during their stay in the First World War, in camps, hostels and lodging houses.

Of non-European groups, we can begin by briefly mentioning the Americans, again heavily focused upon London and consisting of a wide variety of mostly middle class visitors. The small Chinese community in Britain, which developed mainly from sailors, concentrated particularly upon London and Liverpool, and, to a lesser extent, Cardiff, in the late nineteenth and early twentieth centuries. In London the area of settlement lay in the East End, focused upon Limehouse at the start of the twentieth century, while in Liverpool it initially centred upon 'Pitt Street, hard by the Docks'.[22] The sizes of the Chinese communities in London and Liverpool remained tiny, reaching a peak of 1,194 in the former and 529 in the latter during the 1930s.[23]

Black people in Britain during the late nineteenth and early twentieth centuries, like the Chinese, consisted to a considerable extent of sailors, also settled in ports, including Cardiff, Liverpool, Bristol, and North and South Shields. In London settlement focused especially upon the East End. Similar statements can be made about Indians, although, as we shall see in the discussion of socioeconomic structure, both Black and Asian communities consisted of more than just sailors. Concluding this section on geographical distribution with Gypsies, David Mayall has indicated that 'London and the surrounding districts remained the undisputed heart of the travelling population'[24] throughout the nineteenth century.

Can we reach any conclusions about the geographical distribution of immigrants in nineteenth century Britain? In the first place, as previously mentioned, the overwhelming focus remained London, where around 50 per cent of many communities resided. Explanations for this situation would include the opportunities available for economic newcomers, while for refugees it represents the centre of the political world. We can also point to the role of chain migration, which swells London communities out of proportion. Apart from London, we have seen that the other important areas of settlement consist of major northern cities, particularly Manchester and Liverpool, but also Leeds and Glasgow, where, again, we would have to point to economic opportunities. With both Jews and Germans, settlements developed in the transmigratory route across Britain, in places such as Hull. The route also played some role in the growth of major centres such as Liverpool and Manchester. The former city attracted the Irish partly because it was the major staging post into Britain. The explanation for the East End as the major focus within London is similar in the sense that it was very near to the docks where many immigrants first landed.

Age, gender and family structure

If we examine the age, gender and family structure of minorities in Britain, we find that it varies significantly. Apart from the two large groups of the Irish and Jews, we find that an uneven sex structure exists, consisting mainly or overwhelmingly of males. The age composition of first generation immigrants is always uneven because of the fact that they tend to arrive in their twenties over a short period of time and then grow old together. We can expand upon these points by dealing with groupings individually.

We can begin with the Irish, where we have already seen that about half those who moved to England consisted of women. We can also obtain information from various local studies. For instance, in her monograph on York, Frances Finnegan demonstrates that, in 1861, 40 per cent of the Irish were married while 55 per cent were single. She also points to the fact that 'in most age groups in the immigrant community there was a surplus of males to females in each of the post-Famine censuses'. Finnegan has further demonstrated that Irish families were larger than native ones.[25] Meanwhile, in a study of the Bristol census of 1851, David Large showed that nuclear families made up just 37 per cent of Irish households in the city, with 13 per cent consisting of one-parent families, although the more usual pattern involved Irish couples and their children with either their extended family or lodgers. In all, 67 per cent of Irish people over twenty were married, while in 16 per cent of cases the marriage had ended owing to the death of one of the partners.[26] In her study of the Irish in nineteenth century London, Lynn Hollen Lees demonstrates that people between twenty and forty-five 'accounted for 53 per cent of the total Irish born population in 1851'. She further points to the fact that the famine 'forced families to flee the country' which meant that 'the London Irish community in 1851 included a relatively large proportion of children and adults over thirty-four amongst recent immigrants'.[27] Family structure resembled that of the Irish in Bristol, with nuclear families, either existing as such or with more distant relatives and lodgers. Clearly, the Irish in various British cities resembled each other closely, owing to the fairly even sex structure and the migration of family units, meaning that a large percentage of adults were married. The 1901 and 1931 censuses show that Irish males exceeded females in the former, while the trend was reversed in the latter.

A series of surveys carried out by both contemporary writers and historians reveal details about the age, sex and family structure of Anglo-Jewry. Taking figures from the 1901 census, S. Rosenblaum demonstrated a fairly even sex structure for all ages of Russians, who 'may be regarded as resembling most closely the foreign section of the Jewish community', although in Stepney differences existed in the age groups above twenty-five. The effect of immigration upon the age structure of Stepney was 'for the proportion of children to be increased, and for old people to be diminished'. With regard to marriage, Rosenblaum believed that Jews had higher rates than non-Jews.[28] A recent article by Barry Kosmin demonstrated a far higher fertility rate amongst east European than among native Jewish women in the late nineteenth century.[29] In her survey of Jews in east London during the inter-war years, Henrietta Adler pointed to an age structure and family size similar to those of the native population in the area.[30]

The nineteenth century German community revealed a far more uneven age and sex structure than the two family-based groups of the Irish and Jews. According to census statistics, males made up over 60 per cent of Germans throughout the period 1861–1911. During this period, children under fifteen never made up more than 8 per cent of immigrants, although this figure excludes children born in Britain of German parents. With regard to the Italian community in the nineteenth century, Lucio Sponza has demonstrated that Italian women never made up more than 30 per cent of the Italian community in England and Wales between 1861 and 1911, which inevitably meant a high rate of marriage between Italian men and Englishwomen.[31] An even more uneven sex pattern existed amongst the Chinese in the first half of the twentieth century. In 1901, 338 males and 49 females lived in England and Wales, figures which had changed to 1,747 and 187 respectively in 1931. Again this ratio inevitably meant a high proportion of mixed marriages.[32] The picture amongst both Black and Asian groups remained similar throughout the period under consideration.

Employment and class structure

The above discussion of age and sex structure has revealed fundamental differences between small and large groups, a pattern confirmed by an examination of employment and class structure. Once again, the larger minorities reveal a pattern closely connected with that of British society, with a well developed class structure, whereas some of the smaller groupings, such as the Chinese, do not. Scholars such as Lynn Lees and, especially, Bill Williams have realised the fundamental fact that no groups are monoliths, a point which will receive further attention below. We can examine individual minorities.

Most publications on the Irish in nineteenth century Britain, by both contemporaries and historians, have pointed to the fact that the vast majority were either working class or fell within the underclass, or even formed an underclass on their own. Lees, however, has recognised the existence of three groups of Irish people in London. These consisted of a 'small number of middle-class Irish, many

Protestant and culturally similar to the English' who 'chose the metropolis for its professional and educational opportunities', and could fit into native society. The second group was made up of craftsmen who might fit into 'the social world of the London artisan and trade unionist'. However, the largest group consisted of rural labourers, who 'lacked skills and urban experience', moving into London ghettoes.[33]

We can begin with the last group, which existed in all cities inhabited by Irishmen in the first half of the nineteenth century. The development of ghettoes was accelerated by the fact that Irish immigration took place in the early stages of industrialisation, which meant an expanding population in all cities with which available housing resources could not keep pace. The situation particularly deteriorated during the mass Famine influx. Before that time, however, commentators had already pointed to the condition of the Irish in Manchester, who lived in an area of 'Black smoke, polluted rivers, unpaved streets, the smell of pig sties, privies, and open sewers, coupled with the filthy, cramped cellar dwellings with their barren damp interiors.'[34] A similar situation existed in Glasgow, Edinburgh, Greenock and in other Lancashire towns during the 1830s and 1840s (see Document 12), as well as in the St Giles district of London.

The occupations of the Irish in nineteenth century Britain generally remained at the lower end of the social scale and it does not always prove easy to differentiate between underclass and working class activity, just as living conditions do not clearly separate the two. However, we can begin with economic activity which falls below the non-skilled variety, although historians of the Irish have demonstrated a reluctance to tackle what we might describe as the activities of the Irish underclass. Roger Swift, for instance, while admitting the existence of Irish prostitution, plays down its significance, pointing to the fact that it was less common amongst Irish than among English women.[35] Frank Neal, however, has demonstrated that in 1853, Irish women made up 44·3 per cent of prostitutes arrested in Liverpool, and has also shown that the situation remained similar into the second half of the nineteenth century. He further demonstrates the fact that many Irish people in Liverpool, including juveniles, lived by thieving.[36]

The reason for the lack of attention by historians to the concept of an Irish underclass may lie partly in the fact that it merges, without any clear distinction, with the unskilled and skilled working classes. We can best proceed in this discussion on a geographical basis, beginning with London. In the 1850s, Henry Mayhew devoted much attention to the 'street Irish', whom he described as 'both a numerous and peculiar class of people', and 'computed that there are, including men, women, and children, upwards of 10,000'. He continued that 'three-fourths sell only fruit, and more especially nuts and oranges', while others, mostly men, 'deal in fish, fruit and vegetables . . . Some of the most wretched street-Irish deal in such trifles as lucifer-matches, watercresses, &c.'. Mayhew further pointed out that the 'majority of the Irish street-sellers of both sexes beg', meaning that they may also be considered as part of an underclass.[37]

Lees has written more generally about Irish labour in Victorian London, pointing out that the immigrants 'were channeled into the bottom ranks of the capital's social and economic hierarchy', where they struggled for survival but formed a 'vast pool of casual labour upon which such industries as transportation, construction and food distribution depended'. Most 'Irish workers in 1851 worked simply as general labourers'.[38] Skilled trades employing the Irish included shoemaking, which, however, was falling into the category of a sweated industry, where the Irish still worked at the start of the twentieth century. At this time the Irish also continued to work in the same areas of employment as they had done earlier in the century, including casual work, especially as dockers. Navvies further played a role in the development of the London railway network, while other construction workers helped to construct Victorian London (see Document 13).

In the north of England, two occupations in particular have associations with the Irish, in the form of railway work and employment in textiles. In the former, as much as 10 per cent of navvies working in Britain in 1841 were from Ireland,[39] employed in gangs on particular projects, especially in the period 1830–50. In textiles, the Irish worked in towns in both Lancashire and Yorkshire. In Manchester, for instance, they found employment from the 1830s. The range of people employed was wide, including women and children, with an average age of between sixteen and twenty-four. Work time totalled up to thirteen hours per day, while wages 'were incredibly low'.[40] In Bradford, meanwhile, the Irish were involved in a wide variety of textile occupations, including wool combing, hand weaving, worsted spinning, power loom weaving and tailoring. In addition, Irish pedlars also made an existence in Bradford. Pay rates for the Irish textile workers in Bradford, as in Manchester, were low. Elsewhere, in the north of England, the Irish found employment as casual workers in the Cleveland ironstone field, and in a wide variety of occupations in Tyneside.

In Scotland, occupations of the Irish resembled those farther south. In the first place, Irish navvies helped to build the Scottish railways between 1850 and 1880, earning irregular pay. Navvies further assisted in the construction of docks and harbours. In the late nineteenth century the Irish 'took their places in the ranks of the industrial army that laboured at unskilled or semi-skilled jobs', in shipyards, docks, factories, distilleries, potteries and gasworks. In the Lanarkshire coalfield the Irish became employed as miners, making up 42 per cent of employees in Coatbridge in 1861. In the same year they constituted 47·7 per cent of workers in the ironstone industry of Coatbridge.[41]

We can further point to two working class occupations in which the Irish found themselves employed throughout the late nineteenth and early twentieth centuries all over Britain: domestic service and the army. With regard to the former, Finnegan has shown that it formed the second most important field of employment for Irish women in York.[42] In some English towns domestic service 'accounted for more than one-third of occupied Irishwomen',[43] representing the major area of female employment. Irish soldiers joined the British army throughout the years from the late eighteenth to the early twentieth century, so that from 1830 until 1870 'about 50,000 "other ranks" in the British army were usually Irish-born'.[44]

The Irish in Britain therefore worked in a variety of working class occupations. We may see them as representing a reserve army of labour, which could move into work at the bottom end of the social scale in the fields of domestic service, building and the armed services. They differ from all other immigrant communities in Britain between 1845 and 1945 because their number enabled them to move into such a wide range of activities, resembling the work of the domestic working classes.

Another unique feature of the Irish in nineteenth century Britain was the existence of a significant agricultural class in the form of, primarily, seasonal labourers, who worked, as we have previously seen, throughout the country. Most consisted of seasonal migrants. In the 1830s they helped in the hay and corn harvests, sometimes moving into the country alone and sometimes with their children, who would beg. Some worked in hop gardens in Kent from the pre-Famine period. In 1841, 57,651 Irish harvesters entered the country.[45] However, from the 1860s, with the increase in emigration to the United States, the numbers of seasonal Irish labourers in Britain declined, though a slight increase occurred at the turn of the century. Earnings for migrant labourers varied between £4 and £15.[46] Jackson explains the use of such workers by English farmers through 'Increased mechanisation in agriculture, a growing number of large farms specialising in single crop production and the relative immobility of English rural labour.'[47] In some cases, permanent Irish immigrants within Britain worked in agriculture, the best example being the Irish in York, who worked as farm labourers in the production of chicory during the mid-nineteenth century.

Despite the existence of an Irish middle class in Britain, scholars have devoted little attention to it. In some cases social mobility took place, so that costermongers might move into the petty bourgeoisie by becoming shopkeepers. Higher up the social scale, Irish merchants formed an important element in the pre-Famine Liverpool Irish community, living in Abercromby Square, a wealthy part of the city. Furthermore, Irish doctors, lawyers, writers and journalists also lived in nineteenth century Britain. However, 'the Irish presence in these higher reaches of the occupational structure was disproportionately small, whether this disproportion is measured in terms of the occupational structure of the Irish immigrants themselves, or in terms of the occupational structure of the communities in which they settled'.[48] The explanation for this state of affairs lies in the fact that the Irish immigrants entered the country from a less advanced economy with skills which would only suit them for employment at the bottom end of the industrial scale, in contrast to newcomers from Germany, both in the late nineteenth century and during the 1930s, who emigrated with skills from a more advanced economy and could therefore move into employment higher up on the social scale.

Despite the lack of members of the middle classes, the Irish had a fairly complete class structure in Britain, especially as the nineteenth century progressed and social mobility developed. However, the impression given by scholars of the Irish in Britain is of a fairly undifferentiated mass at the bottom of the social scale who would pick up any form of casual labour available. This may be too simplistic a picture, as social variations may well have existed. Nevertheless, it is fair to say that the vast majority of the Irish in Britain fell into the working classes, although we should also recognise the existence of a unique and sizeable element in the form of an agricultural class.

If we move on to the Jewish community in Britain during the period 1815–1945, we find a complex picture, which constantly changes, owing to successive waves of immigration. Like the Irish in Britain, the Jews, partly because of their numbers, develop a complex class structure, which, in contrast to the Irish, reveals a more equal social distribution for much of the period under consideration.

Jews at the bottom end of the social scale resemble the Irish for some of the period, especially during the late nineteenth century, when we have a mass of unskilled labour moving into the clothing trades in east London, Manchester, Leeds and other cities. However, as with the Irish, we can identify groups which would fit into an underclass, consisting of criminals and prostitutes. Beginning with the former, Jews had participated in the receiving and disposing of stolen property during the first half of the nineteenth century. In the late nineteenth century the majority of east European Jews jailed were convicted 'for offences touched with commercial dishonesty, in the style of forgery, receiving stolen goods, fraudulent bankruptcy, adulteration of food, illegal distilling to avoid liquor excise'. Jews hardly ever committed 'crimes of violence – murder, robbery, and rape'.[49] Jews also became involved in prostitution, either as suppliers of women or as prostitutes themselves. With regard to the former, London Jews played a significant role in the export of east European Jewish girls to Buenos Aires, Bombay and Constantinople. Jews further worked as brothel keepers, so that 'Data collected from before the First World War in the East End borough of Stepney shows that 20 per cent of the convictions for brothel-keeping were against Jews.'[50] The Jewish women who became involved in prostitution often fell into this activity immediately upon landing in England, when pimps looking for human flesh would deceive them. However, other

Jewish women became prostitutes subsequently. In many cases, as revealed by average ages of fifteen to twenty-five, this remained a temporary phase.

More 'respectable' Jewish occupations lower down the social scale varied according to the period of time we are considering, although, unlike the Irish, Jews tended to focus far more heavily upon specific activities. A classic early nineteenth century occupation amongst Jews was the peddling of a wide variety of goods, although this had declined in importance by the 1850s. However, Mayhew recognised their continued existence in London in this period, where they sold 'oranges, lemons, sponges, combs, pocket-books, pencils, sealing-wax, paper, many-bladed pen-knives, razors, pocket-mirrors, and shaving-boxes'.[51] However, Mayhew further recognised that Irish costermongers had begun to undercut their Jewish counterparts by this time.

Other Jewish occupations by the mid-nineteenth century included cigar-making, in which sweatshop conditions existed by the 1860s. By this time Jews had already begun to move into the occupations in which they would become particularly prominent at the end of the nineteenth century, in the form of shoemaking and tailoring, although others worked as watchmakers and jewellers.

Late nineteenth century Jewish immigrants particularly focused upon a small number of trades, offering a good example of ethnic employment concentration. In 1901 '42 per cent of all Russian and Polish males in East London, and 54 per cent of females, were engaged in the tailoring trades; a further 13 per cent of the men were employed in boot, shoe and slipper manufacture'. A similar situation existed all over the country, so that by 1911 'about half of all Russians, Poles, and Romanians in England and Wales were engaged in some branch or other of the clothing trades, including footwear and headwear'.[52]

The above Jewish occupations attracted hostile attention from English commentators because of the conditions under which production took place (see Document 14). Many Jews moved into the clothing industries because they were the only trade offering them employment, and therefore faced exploitation by their fellow countrymen, involving long working hours and poor working conditions, although the relevant trades had already begun to move that way before the Jewish influx of the late nineteenth century. Conditions began to improve before the First World War owing to the activities of British trade unions.

During the inter-war years a change took place in working class Jewish occupations. Tailoring still remained the most important East End occupation, but the numbers of both men and women which it attracted had declined, owing to both mechanisation and a depression in the trade. Similar developments took place in other East End Jewish industries in the form of the shoe and boot trades, and cap making. A wide variety of trades in London showed an increase in Jewish participation, including cabinetmaking, cigarette making, engineering, hairdressing, shop work and clerical work.

Throughout Anglo-Jewish history since the readmission, there has always existed a significant middle class, covering various gradations and occupations. During the nineteenth century we can speak of a petty bourgeoisie, especially in provincial towns, which included watchmakers, jewellers and pawnbrokers. Higher up the levels of the bourgeoisie, we can point to manufacturers, many of German origin, of a wide variety of goods, especially textiles, of various sorts, in cities throughout Britain. In addition, Jews also entered the professions during the nineteenth century, as lawyers, dentists, doctors and architects. At the top of the Jewish social ladder there existed what we might describe as a moneyed aristocracy, involved in banking and the stock market. The German Jewish influx of the 1930s brought further middle class Jews into Britain, especially professionals, including academics, lawyers, doctors and architects.

The Jewish class structure was therefore more complete than its Irish equivalent, with less concentration among the lower scales, not simply because of social mobility amongst those who had lived in Britain, and their descendants, over a period of time, but also because of the arrival of already middle class Jews into the country, mostly from Germany, during the nineteenth and early twentieth centuries.

The German class structure resembled the Jewish one in its completeness, and in the fact that it was more equally distributed than its Irish equivalent. At the bottom we can discover a clear underclass, which consisted of the poor, of criminals and of prostitutes. The size of the former varied at different times, according to the prevailing economic conditions, but particular times of distress included the 1880s. The poor also encompassed the old, many of whom relied upon charity. Criminal activities of Germans were similar to those of Jews, connected with financial irregularities rather than violence. Prostitution, meanwhile, was clearly evident amongst Germans, with both pimps and prostitutes. The latter were recruited either upon their arrival in England or lured to the country through misleading advertisements in German newspapers.

The German working classes cover a wide range of activities, although concentration took place in particular trades. A major east London occupation from the eighteenth century was sugar baking, where conditions were extremely harsh (see Document 15), but this activity declined in importance at the end of the nineteenth. Germans also played a role in various occupations connected with clothing, especially in the East End, including skin dying and dressing, tailoring and shoemaking, throughout the nineteenth century, although numbers had declined by the First World War. By the late Victorian years Germans had become important as waiters, especially in London, where they made up about 10 per cent of employees.[53] Seamen, meanwhile, represented a temporary German working-class group in Britain. German brass bands were another migratory group, with many simply visiting the country for the duration of the summer months.

By the outbreak of the First World War a significant German petty bourgeoisie had developed in England, particularly in the field of small business, notably hairdressing, baking and butchering. In all of these, many Germans would begin their career working as cheap labour in the shop of one of their compatriots, before making enough money to establish their own business. Another occupation which we can describe as petty bourgeois is clerical work, in which Germans became important, particularly as foreign correspondence clerks, at the end of the nineteenth century.

We can also identify other middle class occupations amongst Germans, notably teaching. Within this profession, governesses represented a particularly important group, often moving to England because of a lack of employment opportunities in Germany. Male teachers also worked in England. With university expansion in the late Victorian and Edwardian periods, many Germans took up academic posts, especially as teachers of their own language and literature. Germans also played an important role in the development of orchestral music throughout the nineteenth century, either as players or as conductors. Finally, Germans, both Jews and Gentiles, became involved in a wide range of business activities covering fields such as chemicals, banking, steel production and textiles.

The Italian community in Britain also had a developed class structure, although it resembled the Irish minority in a significant concentration at the lower end of the socio-economic scale. Nevertheless, an important shopkeeping group had developed by the end of the nineteenth century. Beginning with the underclass, Sponza has asserted that only small numbers of Italian prostitutes worked in Britain at any one time during the Victorian and Edwardian periods, while the most frequent criminal activity was connected with theft. Unlike Germans and Jews, Italians committed violent crimes to a greater extent, including wounding and assault.[54]

Italians also became involved in itinerant occupations, notably the playing of street music, in which boys often worked under a *padrone*, although individual Italian musicians had lived in England from the early nineteenth century, while others worked as families. Other nineteenth century skilled and unskilled Italian occupations which have attracted attention from historians include itinerant knife grinders, statue posers and figure makers. By 1900 Italians had also moved into the ice cream business, both as makers and as vendors, an activity which continued into the inter-war years, by which time many Italians had established their own businesses. In fact, economic activity in the food trade, including cafe and restaurant proprietorship, represents the development of an Italian petty bourgeoisie by the 1930s.

The other European groups had a varying class structure, often not well developed because of their small size and, in some cases, consisting purely of a bourgeosie. The French colony at the start of the twentieth century, however, was 'anything but wealthy', according to one contemporary article, although a significant number of French shops had previously existed in Bond Street in London. Other French people in early twentieth century London worked 'in City offices and warehouses, in banks, and factories, in workshops and studios, in West-End establishments and shops, in schools and in private families. In all art industries they occupy a prominent position.'[55] In the 1850s, meanwhile, Mayhew had pointed to the existence of French beggars in London (see Document 16), while Sponza has pointed to the fact that the French were the minority most involved in prostitution.[56] In addition, destitute Frenchmen also found their way to London, relying upon assistance from French charities. Female occupations during the late nineteenth century included 'bodice-makers, milliners, seamstresses, dressmakers, laundresses'.[57]

The Swiss community in nineteenth century Britain included merchants who lived in Liverpool, Manchester and Birmingham, and watchmakers. Greeks represented one of the wealthiest communities in nineteenth and early twentieth century Britain, based upon merchants. Russian exiles from the 1917 revolution included both aristocrats and professionals. More working class groups were the Lithuanians, who entered the country in the late nineteenth century, many being attracted to Scottish coalfields, and Belgians, who played a significant role in the First World War munitions industry.

If we move on to examine Black and Asian groups, we cannot find any definite class structure because of the small size of the communities, but some minorities did have a variety of occupations within them. Beginning with Blacks, during the mid-nineteenth century, some 'Negro beggars' lived in London 'and those who attracted attention had mostly come from America – sometimes as stowaways'.[58] Mayhew interviewed some 'Ethiopian serenaders'.[59] The most constant Black group in Britain between 1815 and 1945 consisted of sailors. From the beginning of the nineteenth century Liberian sailors had lived in Liverpool and continued to do so until the First World War. At the end of the nineteenth century a small Black settlement also developed in Canning Town in east London consisting mostly of West Indian seamen. Sailors' communities from Africa and the West Indies developed in other British ports and, despite deportation in 1919, did not disappear. One of the most important was located in Cardiff. Black people also played a role in the British armed forces during both World Wars, while others, as we have seen, were recruited as workers in war production. Throughout the period under consideration, middle class Africans and West Indians lived in Britain, especially students.

A similar range of groups to Blacks existed amongst Indians in Britain between 1815 and 1945. Joseph Salter pointed to the existence of poor and destitute Asians in east London in the mid-nineteenth century, although he may have exaggerated the situation.[60] Many of the people he focused upon were sailors, who also made an appearance in other British ports. Indian students also lived in Britain, as did ayahs, or maids. In addition, individual Indian princes also made appearances in England.

The Chinese community in Britain had a smaller range of occupations, consisting especially of sailors, focused, as we have seen, in east London, Liverpool and Cardiff. However, after the First World War they increasingly became involved in laundry work, while others began to open Chinese restaurants. Furthermore, as with most groups, Chinese students also lived in Britain.

We can conclude this discussion with a consideration of the activities of Gypsies, which David Mayall has put under four headings. First, 'the sale of goods not made by the travellers (horses, fruit, vegetables, pots, pans, needles, pins, jewellery)'. Horse dealing particularly attracted the attention of contemporary commentators. Second, 'the offer of services such as tinkering, knife- and scissor-grinding, umbrella-repairing, chair-bottoming and entertaining'. Third, seasonal agricultural labour. And, fourth, 'the provision of goods and services largely the monopoly of the Gypsies (pegs, baskets, beehives, fortune-telling) incorporating traditional rural crafts and long established skills'.[61] Unlike some of the other groups considered above it proves difficult to construct any class structure for gypsies.

Conclusion

The above discussion leads to various conclusions about the structure of immigrant communities in Britain between 1815 and 1945. In the first place, we need to reiterate the importance of size, which determines a variety of other issues, including gender and family structure and social make-up, although the latter also depends upon other factors. Smaller groups tend to remain isolated, focused upon a more limited number of occupations and male-based, while larger ones are more family-based. However, even minorities such as the Germans, Irish and Jews also tended to work in a limited number of trades.

We might ask whether minorities played any particular role in the British economy during the period under consideration. Can we consider them as a reserve of cheap labour, exploited by

British industry? If we examine the Irish, there exist grounds for such an assertion, as we have seen from the range of basically unskilled occupations in which they became involved. We can put forward similar views with regard to those minorities employed in British shipping as sailors. However, other groupings, such as the Germans and Jews, prove more problematic, in the sense that the exploitation took place by their fellow countrymen, although they obviously operated within the British industrial system, within which labour at the bottom end of the social scale was the only form of employment available.

Nevertheless, the fact that middle class members of some communities existed demonstrates the fact that the concept of a more cheap immigrant labour force proves problematic. Especially in the case of Germans, but also in that of Jews, Swiss and Greeks, many of them entered the country as businessmen and professionals, remaining distinct from any working class, whether the English working class or that of their own community. In the case of the larger minorities the class structure was as rigid as that of English society, a point further illustrated in the next chapter.

Notes

1 Graham Davis, *The Irish in Britain, 1815–1914*, Dublin, 1991, p. 52.

2 John Arthur Jackson, *The Irish in Britain*, London, 1963, p. 11.

3 The figures come from the following sources: V. D. Lipman, *A History of the Jews in Britain since 1858*, Leicester, 1990, pp. 12–13, 205; *idem*, *A Social History of the Jews in England*, London, 1954, p. 99; *idem*, 'A Survey of Anglo-Jewry in 1851', *Transactions of the Jewish Historical Society of England*, vol. 17, 1951–2, p. 174; S. Rosenblaum, 'A Contribution to the Study of the Vital and Other Statistics of the Jews in the United Kingdom', *Journal of the Royal Statistical Society*, vol. 68, 1905, p. 554; Geoffrey Alderman, *Modern British Jewry*, Oxford, 1992, pp. 2, 102.

4 David Mayall, *Gypsy-Travellers in Nineteenth Century Society*, Cambridge, 1988, p. 23.

5 Murdoch Rogers, 'The Lithuanians', *History Today*, vol. 35, July 1985, p. 15.

6 Davis, *Irish in Britain*, 1991, p. 54.

7 Lynn Hollen Lees, *Exiles of Erin: Irish Immigrants in Victorian London*, Manchester, 1979, p. 56.

8 Frank Neal, *Sectarian Violence: The Liverpool Experience, 1819–1914*, Manchester, 1988, pp. 9, 11.

9 M. A. Busteed, R. I. Hodgson and T. F. Kennedy (eds), 'The Myth and Reality of Irish Migrants in Mid-Nineteenth Century Manchester: A Preliminary Study', in P. O'Sullivan (ed.), *The Irish World Wide*, vol. 2, Leicester, 1992, p. 26.

10 C. Richardson, 'Irish Settlement in Mid-Nineteenth Century Bradford', *Yorkshire Bulletin of Economic and Social Research*, vol. 20, 1968, pp. 40–57.

11 T. Dillon, 'The Irish in Leeds', *Thoresby Society Miscellany*, vol. 54, 1973, pp. 1–28.

12 Alderman, *Modern British Jewry*, p. 118; H. L. Trachtenberg, 'Estimate of the Jewish Population of London in 1929', *Journal of the Royal Statistical Society*, vol. 96, 1933, p. 96.

13 Panikos Panayi, *The Enemy in our Midst: Germans in Britain during the First World War*, Oxford, 1988, p. 17.

14 Henrietta Adler, 'Jewish Life and Labour in East London', in *New Survey of London Life and Labour*, vol. 6, London, 1934, pp. 271–2.

15 Lipman, *History of the Jews*, p. 15.

16 Bill Williams, ' "East and West": Class and Community in Manchester Jewry, 1850–1914', in David Cesarani (ed.), *The Making of Modern Anglo-Jewry*, Oxford, 1990, p. 16.

17 Ernest Krausz, *Leeds Jewry: Its History and Social Structure*, Cambridge, 1964, p. 6.

18 Kenneth E. Collins, *Second City Jewry: The Jews of Glasgow in the Age of Expansion, 1790–1919*, Glasgow, 1919, p. 69.

19 Lucio Sponza, *Italian Immigrants in Nineteenth Century Britain: Realities and Images*, Leicester, 1988, pp. 322–3; Terri Colpi, *The Italian Factor: The Italian Community in Great Britain*, Edinburgh, 1991, p. 74.

20 Paul Villars, 'French London', in George R. Sims (ed.), *Living London*, vol. 2, London, 1902, p. 133.

21 Claire H. Gobbi, 'The Spanish Quarter of Somers Town: An Immigrant Community, 1820–30', *Camden History Review*, vol. 6, 1978, p. 6.

22 Colin Holmes, 'The Chinese Connection', in Geoffrey Alderman and Colin Holmes (eds), *Outsiders and Outcasts: Essays in Honour of William J. Fishman*, London, 1993, p. 72.

23 K. C. Ng, *The Chinese in London*, London, 1968, p. 6; Maria Lin Wong, *Chinese Liverpudlians: A History of the Chinese Community in Liverpool*, Birkenhead, 1989, pp. 4–5.

24 Mayall, *Gypsy-Travellers*, p. 34.

25 Frances Finnegan, *Poverty and Prejudice: A Study of Irish Immigrants in York, 1840–1875*, Cork, 1982, pp. 72, 73, 74.

26 David Large, 'The Irish in Bristol in 1851: A Census Enumeration', in Roger Swift and Sheridan Gilley (eds), *The Irish in the Victorian City*, London, 1985, pp. 51, 53.

27 Lees, *Exiles of Erin*, p. 49.

28 Rosenblaum, 'Contribution', pp. 526–62.

29 Barry A. Kosmin, 'Nuptiality and Fertility Patterns of British Jewry, 1850–1980: An Immigrant Transition?', in D. A. Coleman (ed.), *Demography of Immigrant and Minority Groups in the United Kingdom*, London, 1982, p. 257.

30 Adler, 'Jewish Life', pp. 283, 294.

31 Sponza, *Italian Immigrants*, pp. 58–9.

32 Ng, *Chinese in London*, p. 9.

33 Lees, *Exiles of Erin*, pp. 53–4.

34 J. M. Werly, 'The Irish in Manchester, 1832–49', *Irish Historical Studies*, vol. 17, 1973, p. 347.

35 Roger Swift, 'Crime and the Irish in Nineteenth Century Britain', in Roger Swift and Sheridan Gilley (eds), *The Irish in Britain, 1815–1939*, London, 1989, pp. 175–6.

36 Frank Neal, 'A Criminal Profile of the Liverpool Irish', *Transactions of the Historic Society of Lancashire and Cheshire*, vol. 140, 1990, pp. 160–99.

37 Henry Mayhew, *London Labour and the London Poor*, London, 1861, 1968 reprint, vol. 1, pp. 104–5.

38 Lees, *Exiles of Erin*, pp. 88, 94, 95.

39 J. H. Treble, 'Irish Navvies in the North of England', *Transport History*, vol. 6, 1973, p. 229.

40 Werly, 'Irish in Manchester', pp. 352–3.

41 A. B. Campbell, *The Lanarkshire Miners*, Edinburgh, 1979, pp. 178, 179.

42 Finnegan, *Poverty and Prejudice*, p. 106.

43 David Fitzpatrick, '"A Peculiar Tramping People": the Irish in Britain, 1801–70', in W. E. Vaughan (ed.), *A New History of Ireland*, vol. 5, Oxford, 1989, p. 642.

44 *Ibid.*, p. 641.

45 Jackson, *Irish in Britain*, p. 75.

46 Davis, *Irish in Britain*, p. 97.

47 Jackson, *Irish in Britain*, p. 75.

48 M. A. G. OTuataigh, 'The Irish in Nineteenth Century Britain: Problems of Integration', *Transactions of the Royal Historical Society*, 5th series, vol. 31, pp. 155–6.

49 Lloyd P. Gartner, *The Jewish Immigrant in England, 1870–1914*, London, 1960, p. 183.

50 Lara Marks, 'Jewish Women and Jewish Prostitution in the East End of London', *Jewish Quarterly*, vol. 34, 1987, pp. 6–11.

51 Mayhew, *London Labour*, vol. 2, p. 118.

52 Alderman, *Modern British Jewry*, p. 121.

53 Panikos Panayi, 'The German Poor and Working Classes in

Victorian and Edwardian London', in Alderman and Holmes, *Outsiders and Outcasts*, p. 66.

54   Sponza, *Italian Immigrants*, pp. 231–51.

55   Paul Villars, 'French London', in George R. Sims (ed.), *Living London*, vol. 2, London, 1902, pp. 133, 134.

56   Sponza, *Italian Immigrants*, p. 329.

57   *Anglo-French Chronicle of Leicester Square*, 10 January 1880.

58   Michael Banton, *The Coloured Quarter*, London, 1955, p. 26.

59   Mayhew, *London Labour*, pp. 190–4.

60   Joseph Salter, *The Asiatic in England: Sketches of Sixteen Years' Work among Orientals*, London, 1873.

61   Mayall, *Gypsy-Travellers*, p. 47.

4

Ethnicity

A wide range of interpretations of ethnicity exist in academic circles, particularly in sociological and anthropological research.[1] For our own purposes we may describe it as the way in which members of a national, racial or religious grouping maintain an identity with people of the same community in a variety of official and unofficial ways. We can identify three main ways in which ethnicity can survive, consisting of: residence patterns, whereby members of the same groups reside together; marriage patterns, in which immigrants and their children marry within their own grouping; and religious and social activity, by which we mean the recreation, although always in a distorted way for immigrants, of church and social life. An examination of these three main ways of maintaining ethnicity provides the main basis of this chapter, although, because of the availability of material and some discussion in the previous chapter, the bulk of it focuses upon the last issue.

The reasons for the development of ethnicity amongst particular groups are complex. A classic interpretation comes from Oscar Handlin, one of the pioneers in nineteenth century US immigration history, who wrote of the loneliness of immigrants upon their arrival in the United States when they consequently 'reached for some arm to lean upon'. Therefore 'the newcomers took pains early to seek out those whom experience had made their brothers; and to organize each others' support, they created a variety of formal and informal institutions'.[2] More recent Marxist sociological interpretations have viewed ethnicity as negative, a reaction against the host society. Stephen Castles, examining post-war Europe, has written that 'Becoming a minority is a process whereby dominant groups in society ascribe certain (real or imagined) characteristics to the newcomers, and use these to justify the assignment of specific economic, social and political roles. In response to their experience, migrants and their descendants develop their own cultures and institutions, and perceive themselves as distinct groups within society.'[3] It would be difficult to accept fully the latter interpretation for nineteenth century and early twentieth century Britain, although we can recognise elements of Castles's statement as containing elements of truth. We can make the same comment about Handlin's somewhat romanticised words.

We cannot simply speak of one ethnicity which holds all members of a minority together, for a variety of reasons. First, in the context of nineteenth century Britain, we have to place all developments against the background of the existence of a capitalist social structure, as we saw in the previous chapter. Therefore, amongst the larger groups which developed in Britain during this period, we need to recognise that all ways of maintaining ethnicity, whether in the form of residence and marriage patterns, or in the development of institutions, took place upon a class basis. In addition, we need to recognise that different ethnicities develop because of the different origins of members of a particular grouping. Amongst the Irish and Germans we have to point to both Protestants and Catholics. More complicated still are Jews, who divide along grounds of national origin as well as according to their particular Jewish sect.

However, we may also speak of an ethnic identity which holds all members of a particular group together, and which transcends boundaries of class and religion. This applies to larger groups. Apart from the fact that the various communities might form a whole through language and religion, we can also point to the fact that those at the higher end of the social ladder recognised the existence of members of the same group lower down by the provision of philanthropy.

Residence and marriage patterns

In a study of ethnicity amongst Germans in mid-nineteenth century New York City, Stanley Nadel demonstrated that two fundamental ways in which immigrants and their descendants maintained their ethnicity consisted of their residence patterns, whereby they lived in particular blocks, and in their marriage patterns, involving the matching of most individuals to fellow Germans, and even Germans from the same state, down to the third generation.[4] This section will attempt to examine the extent to which this happened amongst groupings in nineteenth century Britain, although a problem exists with regard to lack of research in these areas.

Before moving forward we can discuss the importance of residence and marriage patterns for ethnicity. With regard to the first of these, we essentially mean the development of immigrant neighbourhoods, whose importance lies in the fact that they allow the development of ethnicity upon a local level. This ethnicity demonstrates itself both in the continued use of language and in the development of businesses, churches and cultural organisations in the particular area because 'the costs in time and money of movement within the cities of the nineteenth and early twentieth centuries tended to confine such community life to persons who shared a particular neighbourhood'.[5] The importance of marriage by members of minorities within their own community demonstrates itself in two ways. In the first place, it increases the likelihood of first generation immigrants themselves participating in the activities of their own community, in contrast to those who marry English partners and whose chances of falling into the norms of native society rise. At the same time, the likelihood of the children of immigrants continuing the religion and cultural norms of their parents increases greatly.

As mentioned previously, little research has been carried out into residence and marriage patterns amongst minorities in recent British history, but we can examine such results as exist, beginning with residence patterns. In the previous chapter, we saw that most minorities tended to focus upon particular areas of cities. In this section we can briefly examine some of these areas. The two communities whose local settlement patterns have received most attention are the Irish and the Italians. With regard to the former, most attention has focused upon Liverpool and Manchester. Both Colin Pooley and Frank Neal have examined the Irish. Pooley has pointed out that during the mid-nineteenth century, 'The Irish core-area was clearly in north-central Liverpool, an area of mainly high-density, sub-standard housing, which formed a low-status zone in which, from traditional "ghetto" models of migrant location, the presence of a minority group might be predicted.'[6] Neal, meanwhile, again dealing with the mid-nineteenth century, has examined settlement in Liverpool in more detail, providing statistics of settlement in political wards and even within individual streets. In the Vauxhall ecclesiastical district Chisenhale Street had an Irish population of 82·5 per cent, while in the North End, Harrison Street had an 80 per cent Irish population. Numerous other streets contained more than 50 per cent Irish.[7]

At least two studies of Manchester have dealt in detail with residence patterns. Steven Fielding has demonstrated that the major concentration focused upon north Manchester, a process which continued until the outbreak of the Second World War, when 30 per cent of the population of Moston consisted of Irish.[8] A more detailed study by M. A. Busteed *et al.* has focused upon residence in a particular area of Manchester, using the 1851 census, just to the north-east of the city centre. They have shown that Irish immigrants made up 42·2 per cent of the population of this area. Out of eighty-nine streets studied, forty-one had an Irish majority. Some of these had Irish populations of over 75 per cent.[9] Whether a similar situation developed for Irish communities in other parts of the country seems difficult to establish in the light of an absence of detailed census analyses, although it seems highly likely.

Much work has been produced upon the Italian community of London. Sponza has demonstrated that for most of the nineteenth century it focused upon a few streets, bounded by Holborn Hill, Saffron Hill, Gray's Inn Lane and Darrington Street.[10] Within this area lived Italians involved in a variety of occupations who were able to participate in the cultural activities of their communities. A similar situation developed in Ancoats, the main area of Italian settlement in Manchester.

German settlement in nineteenth century London also remained concentrated, especially in the East End. Even here, particular focuses existed in Whitechapel, St George's in the East and Mile End. During the second half of the nineteenth century movement took place out of the core inner East End, farther out to other areas of east London. One notable factor about German life in London from the end of the eighteenth century is the way in which churches followed the geographical movement of populations themselves, from the City to the East End, and even farther out in east London, illustrating the importance of geographical concentration for the pursuit of ethnic activities.

If we examine marriage patterns amongst immigrants in nineteenth and early twentieth century Britain, we have even more difficulties with regard to lack of research. We have already seen in the previous chapter that marriage to partners of the same group tended to take place amongst the larger minorities, with a large proportion of women, in contrast to the smaller communities, predominantly male, whose members were forced to marry native women. Thus we can suggest that the Irish and Jewish communities could more easily continue their ethnicity into future generations, although even in the latter radical assimilation often took place amongst richer newcomers throughout the period since the readmission in the mid-seventeenth century.

Ethnic organisations

Residence and marriage patterns represent a way in which immigrants maintained their ethnicity, as well as an enabling factor which would allow the development of ethnic organisations. The latter cover a wide range of activities, both formal and informal. Among the formal, the most important consists of religion, which is usually imposed from above, to a greater or lesser degree, either by members of the same community or by British missionaries working in inner city areas in their attempt to 'save souls'. Churches further act as a focus for educational and philanthropic activity amongst ethnic communities, although both of these can develop independently of religion. In all cases, ethnicity imposed from above plays a fundamental role in the solidarity of a community, although as it is official it points immigrants in particular directions. Religion, whether from the community itself, or from British society, represents the most important way in which ethnicity is maintained, existing amongst virtually all communities, no matter what their size.

Other ethnic organisations tend to develop from below, revolving around cultural, trade union and political activity. Culture covers a variety of miscellaneous activities, but the main function of many cultural groupings is simply to perpetuate the perceived traditions of the country of origin, whether through sport, theatre, dancing or any other form of activity. Class plays a fundamental role in the cultural activity which a member of a minority pursues, so that it is rare, if not impossible, for members of a minority from different classes to become members of the same club, as we will see below. Some possibility exists in politics, especially of a radical nature, where both the middle classes and the working classes of a particular minority may meet. Politics can cover much of the political spectrum, from nationalist groupings to left-wing ones. For many refugees, participation in a political cause in their land of exile represents the only form of ethnic activity available to them. Trade union activity is obviously based upon class lines, although we should also mention professional bodies in this context, which represent middle class rather than working class interests.

Clearly the diversity of ethnic organisations re-emphasises the point about the wide range of ethnicities which existed during the period 1815–1945. Immigrants made a conscious decision about which bodies they would join, according to their class, occupational, political and religious status, although in cases of ethnicity from above they were directed towards particular areas, as we have seen. The rest of this chapter will proceed along the lines of examining religion and philanthropy, cultural bodies and political activity.

Religion and philanthropy

Several historians of ethnicity in the United States have viewed religion as the most important factor in maintaining identity. Handlin believed that 'The very process of adjusting immigrant ideas to the conditions of the United States made religion paramount as a way of life',[11] a position supported by Will Herberg, who believed that the 'first concern of the immigrants . . . was with their churches'.[12] Frederick C. Luebke, referring to the Germans in the United States during the nineteenth century, claimed that they 'identified themselves first of all as Catholics, Lutherans, Evangelicals, Mennonites, or Methodists, and only secondarily (sometimes only incidentally) as Germans'.[13] This position seems extreme, although we may agree that, with many groups, loyalty to religion played just as important a role as maintaining links with the country of origin. For Jews this was clearly fundamentally important, although the religion of Russian immigrants in the late nineteenth century differed from that of native Jews in various ways, tied to the traditions in the countries in which the religion of Russian and English Jews had developed. For some groups, and individuals within those groups, religion may have represented the only way in which to maintain ethnicity. Perhaps the most accurate statement on religion and ethnicity comes from Jay P. Dolan, who wrote that immigrants to the United States reproduced 'the type of religion with which they were familiar in the old country; for some it was an active spiritual life centered on the parish; for others it was an indifferent attitude toward religion, and the immigrant parish was hard-pressed to change these patterns of tradition'.[14]

We can best proceed in this discussion by examining religion amongst individual groups, beginning with the Irish. Immediately, we need to recognise the existence of both Catholics and Protestants. Commencing with the former, we can make a few comments about religion in Ireland. Graham Davis points to the 'very high level of attendance at places of religious worship in modern Ireland', although he also mentions the fact that attendance varied from one parish to another. But the effect of the Irish famine was to increase religious observance, at the expense of belief in superstition and witchcraft.[15] This religious observance, as well as being spiritual, also focused upon adherence to Ireland, creating a 'loyalty to Faith and Fatherland'.[16]

The influx of the Irish into Britain, especially after the Famine, had a profound impact upon the existing Roman Catholic Church within the country, as the number of Catholic Irish may have totalled 1·2 million. 'Between 1800 and 1870 it was transfigured from being a small, proud, rich, and unpopular body to become a large, prudent, poorer, and popular body, with a vast majority of Irish adherents.'[17] Initially, the Catholic Church in Britain displayed reluctance about ministering to the Irish poor, and a lack of interest was demonstrated by English priests. Part of the initial failure to meet the spiritual needs of the Irish immigrants lay in the demands caused by the scale of the influx, especially during the Famine, which meant that human, physical and financial resources were 'intolerably over-strained',[18] especially in terms of the number of priests available, as well as in terms of a shortage of money. As the century progressed, and these problems lessened, Catholic churches grew up in Irish districts, as did schools. Missionary organisations, such as the Marist and the Catholic Young Men's Society, played a large role in the early stages of the Irish influx. If we turn to rates of attendance at services, Graham Davis has given one of 50 per cent, although he admits that this varied from one geographical location to another and at different time periods.[19] All these themes can be illustrated in further detail if we examine religion amongst the Irish in geographical areas.

We can start with London, which began to face problems with regard to the number of Catholics from as early as 1816, although only one new church had been built until 1840. During the following decade the number of Irish in the capital, including those born there, increased from 100,000 to 150,000. However, only 40,000 attended Sunday morning mass on census Sunday in 1851.[20] Missionary work to the Irish in the capital took place with the help of funding from rich London Catholics, foreign ambassadors and contributions from abroad. The Jesuits were one of the bodies which took part in missionary work, while Father Lucas led an Irish mission. Both nuns and monks played a role in the spread of religion to the newly arrived Irish immigrants. 'When a colony of unchurched Irish was discovered, either the Bishop or the local clergy would send a priest there to revive interest in religion.'[21] Initially, priests would hold services in attics or sheds because of the lack of churches. With regard to attendance, Lees doubts the level of commitment of most Catholics, speaking of two Irish populations: 'a minority of active participants and the majority, whom the priests saw irregularly between the ceremonies consecrating birth and death or not at all'.[22] The leakage from the Church increased with the passage of the century.

As mentioned above, with regard to the role of religion generally, the Catholic Church in London acted as a focus for a variety of activities including teetotal societies and infant schools. As Lees has pointed out: 'Roman Catholic culture as it touched the Irish thus contained heavy doses of social discipline. But it also helped migrants to adapt to urban society . . . Catholic relief organizations helped the poor to survive bad winters and periods of long unemployment. Church schools and clubs taught reading and sometimes offered job training.'[23]

The Roman Catholic Church also played an important role in Liverpool and Manchester. By the 1870s the former contained 'twenty-three Catholic churches, ten convents, and seven monasteries', supported 'by the zealous charity of the Irish people', both rich and poor. The Catholic population also provided education for about one in eight of its children (see Document 17). During the inter-war years sixteen Catholic parishes existed in the northern dockland area of the city, whose population totalled 95,000, and the number of priests varied from seventy to seventy-five. In addition, 'the Catholic Church in Liverpool had, by the 1920s, effectively established a micro-welfare state within the city. Between 1926 and 1939 there were twenty-four social and charitable organisations administered by Irish nuns'.[24] These included schools, nurseries and hostels. Other philanthropic organisations included the Catholic Women's League and the Catholic Social Guild.

The Catholic Church had also developed a similar complex of organisations in Manchester during the nineteenth and early twentieth centuries. Just before the outbreak of the First World War, 13 per cent of children in the city were taught at Catholic schools. In addition, the Catholic Church also established organisations to control its youth, including the Catholic Lads' Clubs and the Catholic Boys' Brigade movement. Steven Fielding has also pointed to the importance of Catholic street processions, with the numbers participating reaching a peak during the late 1930s. The number of Catholics in Manchester rose from 98,000 in 1890 to 130,000 in 1931, although the proportion of those born in Ireland declined. In 1900 thirty-one parishes existed in the city, although attendance varied from one location to another.[25]

One of the greatest concentrations of Catholics in Britain lay in Scotland, where numbers increased from 126,000 in 1841 to 500,000 by the outbreak of the First World War, about 11 per cent of the population.[26] As in other parts of Britain, as well as providing spiritual leadership the Church offered education and other philanthropic assistance to its community. In Dundee two Catholic churches and three schools existed in the early 1860s, both of which figures doubled within ten years. By the outbreak of the First World War, the Church had also established various welfare bodies, including a nursery, and a Home for Catholic Working Boys.[27] Scotland also acted as one of the main centres of attraction for Irish Protestants, although one of the major manifestations of ethnicity, the formation of Orange Orders, is discussed below under political groupings.

When we turn to Jewish ethnicity in Britain, we have to recognise the fact, as mentioned above, that it incorporates both natives and immigrants to a greater extent than any other community. In contrast to other groupings, the fact of being a Jew, rather than, or as well as, an immigrant represented the main driving force behind the development of ethnicity. The actual establishment of a synagogue proved fundamental in the creation of a Jewish community. We should also reiterate the fact that we cannot speak of a single Jewish ethnicity, but differing ones, as the following discussion will demonstrate.

At the beginning of the nineteenth century the main division was between Sephardic Jews, originating in the Iberian Peninsula, and Ashkenazi Jews from eastern Europe. By that time the latter outnumbered the former. However, the Sephardim had developed a wide range of charitable activities from the late seventeenth century, focused upon their base in London. With the passage of time, Sepahardim were overtaken more and more by Ashkenazim.

The latter were served by forty-one synagogues in the United Kingdom by the early 1860s, and the philanthropic institutions connected with them. By this time, a centralised structure had developed amongst the Ashkenazim. One of the instruments of this consisted of the Chief Rabbinate, established in the 1840s, which unified religious practice and provided Jewish popular education. In 1850 the Jewish community 'had a network of voluntary day schools in London and the main provincial centres, with over 2,000 pupils and 36 teachers'.[28] Financial support came in the form partly of large donations from rich Jews and partly of smaller ones from a wider section of the community. The United Synagogue, established in 1870, also played a centralising role. However, some minor synagogues or *hebroth* remained independent even during the mid-nineteenth century.

This development intensified with the mass influx from eastern Europe, from the 1880s. The newcomers established *hebroth* or *chevrot* 'in any back- or upstairs-room, attic, or hut that could be found for the purpose', as they could not afford anything better. These grew up in the communities which developed all over the country. Twenty came into existence in Liverpool, while in London scores appeared. Alderman lays much stress upon the fact that the newcomers avoided established synagogues, setting up their own welfare and educational institutions, as well as places of worship.[29] In addition, they also had their own rabbis amongst them. The reluctance to participate in the activities of established Jewish communities lay at least partly in the fact that the newcomers faced hostility from established Anglo-Jewry. This animosity played a role in the establishment of the Federation of Synagogues in 1887, which united the *chevrot*, and caused friction with the United Synagogue.

During the inter-war years the complexity of Jewish religious life intensified, owing to two developments. First, the influx of refugees from Nazism, whose entry into the country led to the establishment of new Orthodox communities in north-west London and Manchester. In addition, Hasidic Jews, who had entered the country before 1914, began to organise themselves to a greater extent. More generally, in London 139 synagogues existed. The *chevrot* also remained in large numbers. At least 15,000 pupils attended Jewish schools in the capital, excluding those who attended institutions simply for religious instruction.[30]

We should also mention the Board of Deputies of British Jews, a nationwide organisation, established in 1859 for the purpose of relieving poor Jewish immigrants. Its membership included the representatives of London synagogues. During the second half of the nineteenth century the workload of the organisation increased, owing to the influx of European Jews and economic recession. The organisation continued to exist throughout the nineteenth and twentieth centuries.

The German communities in nineteenth century Britain developed a religious life which played a central role in the maintenance of ethnicity. Like the Jewish minority, various groups existed within the country, divided into Protestants, Catholics and Jews. The first of these counted the largest numbers, as we can see by beginning our examination in London. By 1800 five German Lutheran or Evangelical churches existed in the capital, one of which, the Court Chapel, disappeared in 1901. The others consisted of the Hamburg Lutheran Church, which possessed one of the largest congregations (see Document 18) and moved to Dalston in east London, but outside the East End, in 1871; St George's in Little Alie Street, in Whitechapel; St Paul's, also situated in Whitechapel; and St Mary's in Cleveland Street, St Pancras. Other churches appeared in new areas of German settlement, including those which served the middle class congregations in Forest Hill and Denmark Hill in south London. In addition, we can also mention Christ's Church in Kensington, which held its first service in 1904, and the Evangelical Church in Islington founded in 1857.

Other German churches appeared for short periods of time and faded away. We can also mention the Mission among the German Poor in London, whose committee consisted of the German pastors of London, and which aimed at spreading Christian knowledge among the German population (see Document 19).

During the nineteenth century Protestant churches also developed amongst the tiny German communities which existed throughout the country. Manchester, for instance, had three German churches at the end of the nineteenth century, divided upon class and geographical lines. In Liverpool, a German church came into existence at the end of 1840s based upon transmigrants, sailors and a more established community. A similar situation developed in Hull. Other cities with German churches included Sunderland, Bradford, Edinburgh and Birmingham. The German Protestant community in Britain also created a central organisation in the form of the Association of German Evangelical Congregations in Great Britain and Ireland in 1904.

The individual churches invariably had a variety of institutions connected with them, including schools and women's committees. Finance for their establishment came from a range of sources, including wealthy English and German philanthropists. The foundation of a church had almost a symbolic significance, indicating that a German community had established itself and could raise the funds to support a place of worship.

The German community in Britain had also developed a vast philanthropic network by the end of the nineteenth century, consisting of charities, notably the Society of Friends of Foreigners in Distress and the German Society of Benevolence, together with old people's homes, schools and orphanages. Many of these, together with the churches, survived the upheaval of the First World War to continue in existence during the inter-war years.

Only one German Catholic church existed in Britain throughout the course of the nineteenth century, St Bonifacius, established in London in 1809, although other German Catholics may have attended Irish immigrant churches. By the start of the twentieth century St Bonifacius had become involved in educational, missionary and philanthropic activity. German Jews tended to move into congregations with other Ashkenazim during the course of the nineteenth century, although they did count enough numbers to establish their own synagogues in Dundee and Bradford.

Smaller European communities also set up places of worship in the nineteenth and early twentieth centuries. For instance, St Peter's was established for the Italian minority in Clerkenwell in 1864. Two Italian schools existed in London in the first half of the nineteenth century, while the Italian Benevolent Society was formed in 1861, and continued to exist until the Second World War and beyond. By the end of the 1930s eleven schools in London were offering tuition in Italian to 1,300 pupils.[31]

The history of Greek settlement in Britain has always been accompanied by the establishment of a Greek Orthodox church, the first one existing from 1677–1682. In the ninetenth century a new one was set up in Finsbury Circus in the City of London, and moved to another location within the City twelve years later (see Document 20). A permanent church was subsequently opened in 1879 in the form of St Sophia in Bayswater in west London, with the congregation consisting mostly of wealthy Greeks (see Document 21). Places of worship for the Greek Orthodox community also came into existence in Liverpool, Manchester and Cardiff during the course of the nineteenth century.

Among other immigrant groups which had places of worship in London at the turn of the century, we can point to Russians, Dutch, Swedes, French Catholics and French Protestants, Swiss, Danes, Norwegians and Finns. We can also mention the establishment of an Armenian church in London in 1922, 'mainly through a large donation from Calousta Gulbenkien, a wealthy Armenian businessman'.[32] Many of the London European communities had their own charities by the mid-nineteenth century, including French Protestants and Roman Catholics, and the Dutch.

We can also point to the activities of native missionary societies, notably the London City Mission, which visited virtually all immigrant groups in the capital during the course of the nineteenth century. The Church Missionary Society played a leading role in the establishment in 1885 of 'The Strangers' Home for Asiatics, Africans, South Sea Islanders and others occasionally residing in the Metropolis'.[33] However, we cannot really say that these religious institutions assisted in the maintenance of ethnicity.

Clearly, religion has played an important role in the maintenance of ethnicity for most groups of any size which resided in Britain during the nineteenth and twentieth centuries. As we have seen, we may view the construction of a place of worship as symbolic of the establishment of an ethnic community in a particular district. For all European groups, churches and synagogues have followed their settlement throughout the country. In addition, a complex of philanthropic and educational activities follows these places of worship, as does philanthropic activity independent of them.

Cultural organisations

For some ethnic groupings in Britain, notably the Jews and the Irish, religion served as a more important axis around which activity revolved than for others. For Germans the concept of culture played a more important role, a concept which needs some definition. Culture basically refers to an adherence to the perceived traditions of the country of origin, recreated, usually in a distorted fashion, primarily through the establishment of clubs, although other activities can also play a role. As mentioned previously, clubs operated along class lines, with little mixing between the bourgeoisie and proletariat of any particular ethnic group. More documentation survives upon middle class than upon working class bodies, although the latter almost certainly outnumbered the former among most minorities of any size. We can tackle different groups individually.

Beginning with the Irish, we can see that much of their social activity was controlled from above, in the sense that the Roman Catholic Church played an important role. For instance, we can point to the formation of Catholic Lads' Clubs and the Catholic Boys' Brigade, which, as previously mentioned, were well represented in Manchester, and in which the Church and philanthropy played a significant role, as they aimed at controlling young Catholics. Similarly, the Catholic Young Men's Society, founded in 1850, had religious and educational purposes, with branches in Scotland, England and Ireland. However, by the end of the nineteenth century there had developed a 'full spectrum of immigrant associations dedicated to the cultivation of Irish music and song, Irish debating and literary clubs, Gaelic League branches'.[34] Liverpool had a middle class Catholic club as early as 1844. In addition, we can also mention St Patrick's Day celebrations and, more informally still, rituals surrounding death, in the form of the Irish wake.

As we have repeatedly stressed, religion plays a fundamental role in the maintenance of Jewish ethnicity, and, as with the Irish, philanthropy can control social activity, as we can see with the formation in the late nineteenth century of orgnaisations such as the West Central Jewish Girls' Club and the Jewish Lads' Brigade, supported by wealthy Anglo-Jewish philanthropists, as 'vehicles for the transmission of British values'[35] to newly arrived east European Jewish children.

However, in addition to these bodies we can also point to more purely cultural ones, particularly those which attracted middle class members. Throughout the nineteenth and early twentieth centuries most Jewish communities had literary societies. That in Newcastle, for instance, came into existence in 1903, folded in World War I, and was reformed in 1923 as the Jewish Literary and Social Society. This put on a lecture series and also had a dramatic section connected with it. Even a community as small as Merthyr had a Literary and Social Society from the mid-nineteenth century, as did the larger Jewish population in Glasgow. In Cardiff, meanwhile, by the 1890s there existed a Jewish Literary and Musical Institute and a Hebrew Social Club. In London countless organisations of a literary nature existed in the late nineteenth century. Jewish refugees from Nazism engaged in cultural activities of their own. For instance, they established an organisation called the Free German League of Culture in 1938, 'with the aim of preserving a free and humanist German culture, of promoting mutual understanding between the exiles and the British population, and of looking after the social and cultural needs of the emigres'.[36]

For German and other European minorities in Britain during the nineteenth and early twentieth centuries, religion played a less important role in the maintenance of ethnicity, allowing cultural activity to play a larger part. Amongst Germans hundreds of clubs must have existed during the Victorian and Edwardian years, catering for both the middle and the working classes and for a wide variety of interests, reflecting the situation of German communities in other parts of the world. German clubs, or *Vereine*, in London were described in an article by Count Armfelt in 1903, who outlined the activities of both working class and middle class organisations (see Document 22). Charles Booth's survey of London at the end of the nineteenth century identified a mixture of working class and middle class bodies in the East

End, including the United German Club, with 400 members in 1881, the Sonnenscheine and Niremberg's in Whitechapel, the German Club and a German Bakers' Club in St George's, and a German Social Club, as well as a German Dramatic Club in Shoreditch.[37] In addition, clubs frequented by the highest stratum of German society in Britain existed in cities throughout the country. In London these included the British Wagner and Goethe Societies, the German Athenaeum, and the Turnverein, or German Gymnastic Society. Manchester also had a Turnverein, as well as a Liedertafel, or song society. Bradford contained a Schillerverein and a Liedertafel, while in Liverpool there existed a Deutscher Club and a Deutscher Liederkranz.

The Italian community in Britain also developed clubs and societies between 1815 and 1945. The longest lasting was the Mazzini–Garibaldi Club, founded in 1864. By the end of the nineteenth century it 'formed the heart of social activity for men of the Clerkenwell community'.[38] Throughout the late nineteenth and early twentieth centuries numerous smaller clubs existed in the main areas of Italian settlement in London, where drinking and gambling took place. Italian cultural activity also developed in Manchester and Glasgow.

The Swiss community in London supported a large number of clubs by the inter-war years. One of the most substantial of these was the City Swiss Club, founded in 1856, whose membership rose from 138 in 1877 to an average of 255 during the inter-war years.[39] The other major Swiss club was the Swiss Mercantile Society, which served as the centre of a variety of activities (see Document 23). Further Swiss bodies which existed during the 1920s included the Swiss Alpine Club, the Union Ticineux, the Union Helvetia, the Schweizerbund, the Swiss Institute, the New Helvetia Society, the Swiss Choral Society, the Swiss Gymnastic Society, the Swiss Rifle Association, and the Swiss Club in Birmingham.

Like the Swiss community, the American colony in London developed a wide range of social activities. Histories of Americans in the capital point to the fact that most of the immigrants were middle class, consisting of writers, clergymen, 'lawyers, doctors, businessmen, educators, students, housewives, schoolteachers, actors, health seekers, society women, youthful wanderers'.[40] Among the best known societies were the Atlantic Union, which aimed at bringing Americans and Britons together, and the Society of American Women in London, whose object was 'the promotion of social intercourse between American women, and to bring together women who are engaged in literary, artistic, scientific, and philanthropic pursuits, with the view of rendering them helpful to each other and helpful to Society'.[41] However, there was probably less of a need for ethnicity among Americans than among other minorities because they could move into English society more easily, owing to close linguistic and cultural ties. We can say the same about Canadians, although an organisation called the Canada Club existed from 1810, with a membership which reached a peak of 545 in 1930.[42]

Smaller minorities also participated in cultural activities. For instance, we can mention the formation of a club for Greek residents in London in 1909 which aimed at bringing tradesmen and craftsmen together, and providing them with music and lectures, as well as acting as a mutual aid society. For the Russian community of east London one of the most important meeting places consisted of the Russian Library. Among the Chinese community, opium smoking represented a widespread activity in port areas, while students formed their own organisations in the various towns in which they studied.

Political and trade union activity

Political and trade union activity can prove as important as the recreation of culture in the maintenance of ethnicity. As the very reason for refugees' presence in Britain lay in the fact that they had participated in political activities in their own country, they were likely to continue the struggle in their land of exile. We can view this as an ethnic activity both because of the concern with the homeland and because of the fact that the refugees mixed with their countrymen. In addition, economic immigrants also became involved in politics, particularly, in the case of the working classes, that of a radical nature. We might link trade union activity with this, because, like left-wing politics, it stressed working class ethnicity rather than ethnicity which crossed the social spectrum. However, as well as left-wing politics, there also developed nationalistic groupings which had a more obvious connection with the homeland. Members of virtually all minorities became involved in political activity of one sort or another, and we can examine individual groupings in turn.

In the case of the Irish, political activity took a variety of forms. The first of these, which had a sectarian dimension, involved Protestants who joined Orange Orders. The Orange Order came into existence in County Armagh in Ireland in 1795, and branches began to appear in England and Scotland at the start of the nineteenth century, concentrated particularly in Lancashire and Scotland. In Liverpool the Orange Order was established in 1819 and played a large role in the development of the endemic ethnic violence which characterised Liverpool until the outbreak of the First World War. This would involve the attacking of Orange marches by Catholics or a similar opposition to Catholic processions by Orangemen. In addition, the Orange Order played a role in council elections in the city. The organisation did not develop to the same extent in Manchester, owing to the smaller number of Irish Protestants in the city. However, lodges existed there from the start of the nineteenth century, and the 'country's first Orange riot also took place in the city in 1807'. In 1888 a major disturbance took place in Manchester, but only 200 active Orangemen lived in the city by the 1920s.[43]

The first Orange lodge in Scotland appeared in Maybole in 1800, supported by Irish migrant weavers, who played a large role in the early development of Orangeism throughout the country in the first half of the nineteenth century. By 1835 the movement had spread to both small and large centres, including Paisley, with two lodges, and Glasgow, which counted twelve. The Orange Order attracted mostly working class immigrants, who viewed it 'as a way of maintaining a distinct identity, of distinguishing themselves from the Catholic Irish'.[44] As in Lancashire, sectarian conflict developed in Scotland, especially in Glasgow. The Orange Order continued to exist into the inter-war years, exercising a strong influence on Scottish Protestant working class politics.

Roman Catholic political activity in Britain from 1815 to 1914 proves more complicated, partly because Catholics became more heavily involved in English working class politics. However, we can point to more straightforward Catholic Irish activity in the form of nationalist movements which existed in various forms during the course of the nineteenth century. For instance, in 1840 a Repeal Association was established to campaign for the abolition of the

Act of Union between Britain and Ireland. In 1873 the Home Rule Confederation of Great Britain came into existence. In addition, a more extreme grouping committed to violence also existed in Britain during the late nineteenth century, in the form of the Irish Republican Brotherhood, whose main geographical concentration in Britain lay in Lancashire, which held the largest number of branches.

In Liverpool, the Irish Nationalist Party played a role in governing the city, owing to the large number of Irish immigrants who lived there. At the beginning of the twentieth century it had 'at various times, 10,000 members in 17 active branches, shared the government of the city for three years, formed the official opposition in the Council as late as 1922 with 23 members, and had the wholehearted support' of the immigrant population.[45] The Irish also had an influence on politics in some of the other areas in which they settled, although it was not so profound. Furthermore, in the first half of the nineteenth century they played a role in the Chartist movement, where two of the leaders, Feargus O'Connor and James Bronterre O'Brien, were Irish, while many Irishmen also made up part of the mass membership.

The Jewish community in Britain resembled the Irish in the fact that nationalism, in the form of Zionism, represented a major form of political activity. At the same time, we can also point to activism in more radical politics. We can begin with Zionism. The Zionist Organisation was founded in 1897 with the aim of securing the foundation of an openly recognised and legally secured Jewish homeland. Two years later followed the English Zionist Federation, although prior to this there had existed at least four Zionist organisations with branches in various parts of Britain. The most prominent of these was the Choverei Zion Association, which actually received support from established Anglo-Jewry and east European immigrants, although it did not unify the two groups. By 1914 the English Zionist Federation had fifty branches, thirteen in London, thirty-five in the provinces and two in the colonies. However, Alderman questions the importance of Zionism amongst the East End Jewish working classes before 1914, while accepting that it had grown in influence after World War I.[46] This reflects the growth in importance of Zionism both internationally and within Britain. Referring to the latter, the English Zionist Federation had increased to 30,000 members by 1921, as well as 234 affiliated bodies,[47] including the Federation of Women Zionists of the United Kingdom. In 1928 there followed a University Zionist Federation. Writing in 1949, Paul Goodman commented that 'Zionism has so deeply impregnated Anglo-Jewish thought that, even among most of the erstwhile critics and opponents, it is now, as a whole, taken for granted.'[48]

However, more left-wing Jewish organisations also existed in Britain during the late nineteenth and early twentieth centuries. One of these focused upon the East End and consisted of anarchists revolving around the German exile Rudolf Rocker before the First World War. Before this Jews had also been attracted by socialism, forming their own bodies and joining English organisations. We can also point to Jewish suffragette activity in the form of the Jewish League for Woman Suffrage (see Document 24). In the inter-war years many East End Jews joined the Communist Party as a way of fighting the British Union of Fascists.

The late nineteenth and early twentieth centuries were significant periods for the development of Jewish trade unionism, which evolved on a significant scale in east London, Leeds and Manchester, especially in the tailoring trade. In the first of these towns, 'by the outbreak of World War I some 65 per cent of the organized tailoring work force of London was Jewish, though in total it represented 30 per cent of the whole'.[49] In his study of Leeds, Joseph Buckman rightly put forward the concept that, for newcomers from eastern Europe, the development of trade unions and strikes demonstrated that class solidarity was more important than ethnic identification with Jewish employers.[50]

Political activity amongst Germans in nineteenth century Britain covered the whole range of the political spectrum, despite the fact that most attention has focused upon the left. The groupings on that end of the political spectrum included Young Germany, which established itself in London in 1834. In 1840 there followed the communist German Workers' Educational Association, which had a membership of 300 in 1848 and continued to exist until the First World War. Also in the 1840s the Fraternal Democrats of All Nations unified refugees from a range of European countries. After the failed 1848 revolutions in Germany both liberals and communists returned to Britain. The former set up bodies which included the German Agitation Union of London, the Emigration Club, and German Unity and Freedom. The more left-wing refugees played a role in developments which encompassed a variety of newcomers from Europe, leading to the establishment of the First International in 1864. In the late 1870s and 1880s a series of anarchist clubs developed in London, primarily as a result of the refugees who fled the German Anti-Socialist Laws of 1878. As well as being centres for political activity, the left-wing clubs also offered social and educational benefits. In the years leading up to the First World War, as German nationalism developed, some right-wing pressure groups set up branches in Britain, including the German Colonial Society and the Navy League, the latter of which had representatives in London and Glasgow.

We can also mention German bodies established for members of specific trades, both middle class and working class. For instance, amongst female employees we can point to the Association of German Governesses and to Gordon House, which assisted servants. Both of these acted as employment agencies and received philanthropic support. A German Teachers' Association represented males. For barbers there existed the east London Concordia and the west London International Union of Journeymen Hairdressers in London. The main waiters' associations were the London and Provincial Hotel Employees' Society, Ganymede Friendly Society for Hotel and Restaurant Employees, the London Hotel and Restaurant Employees' Society, and the International Hotel Employees' Society.

The most interesting developments in the political history of the Italian community in London took place during the inter-war years, with the takeover of the institutions of the community by the Fascist government. As early as 1921 the London branch of the *fascio* was founded. In addition, other political organisations came into existence, including the Associazione Nazionale Alpini, a semi-military grouping.

In the middle of the nineteenth century, Polish exiles in London fundamentally concentrated upon political activity. For instance, during the 1840s, some of them joined the Fraternal Democrats, mentioned above, while others played a role in the formation of the Polish Democratic Committee and the Democratic Committee for Poland's Regeneration. Many of these organisations received support from English radicals. During the early 1850s 'there existed several minute Polish socialist societies founded by *emigres* resident in London'. One of these, the Society of the Polish Emigration,

formed the nucleus for the formation of a revolutionary commune.[51] The First World War, just before the foundation of the
Polish state, also represented an important period for political
activity amongst Poles in Britain.

Other east European newcomers also involved themselves in
political activity once they had made their way to Britain. For
instance in 1890 the Society of Friends of Russian Freedom was
established. It 'brought together Russian revolutionaries and radicals and their English sympathisers'[52] and lasted until 1915. It
was one of numerous bodies established by Russian exiles in the
late Victorian and Edwardian years. Lithuanians in Scotland also
established political bodies in the same period. These included a
branch of the Lithuanian Social Democratic Party, set up in 1903,
and the Lithuanian Working Women's Association.

Political activity represented the major way of maintaining ethnicity for Black immigrants in Britain between 1815 and 1945
because it served as the only binding force which could hold
Black people from all over Africa and the West Indies together.
Late nineteenth century organisations included the Anti-Slavery
and Aboriginies' Protection Society, and the African Association.
In 1900 the Pan-African Conference was held in London, with
representatives from Africa, the United States, Canada, the West
Indies and Britain, resulting in the formation of a Pan-African
Association. In the inter-war years the most significant Black
groupings consisted of the West African Students' Union and the
League of Coloured Peoples. The former actually included Africans
from all over the continent amongst its members, as well as West
Indians. It aimed at returning political power to natives in Africa.
The League of Coloured Peoples, established in London in 1931,
had mostly West Indian members, and aimed at improving the
position of its members and of Black people throughout the world.

Conclusion

Ethnic groups in nineteenth and early twentieth century Britain
maintained their ethnicity in a wide variety of ways. The importance of particular activities varied according to factors such as the
importance of religion to an individual group or the reasons for
their presence in Britain. Clearly, religion is fundamental to Jews
whereas politics is just as important to refugees.

We have seen that some ways of maintaining ethnicity came from above, while others originated from below. Among the latter we can include marriage patterns, and trade union, political and cultural activity. Formal ethnicity is really controlled by religion and philanthropy, both of which we may regard as a form of social control by members of a particular community higher up the social scale. However, religious participation can also originate from below, as we can especially see from the *chevrot* which developed in the East End in the late nineteenth century.

Does class solidarity play a more important role for immigrants than ethnic solidarity across social barriers? We can give a categorically positive answer to this question. However, we should first recognise that ethnicity can cross class boundaries, as we can see from philanthropy, although here we must accept that those who give have no contact with those who receive. The overwhelming evidence suggests that ethnicity worked upon a class basis in the class society of Britain in the nineteenth and early twentieth centuries. We can see this in a variety of ways. First, in residence patterns, as middle class members of a community do not live in the same area as the working class members. Second, in marriage patterns it would be unlikely that, for instance, a member of Anglo-Jewry in the late nineteenth century would select an east European immigrant as a partner. Third, in religion, where different residence patterns meant middle class members of a particular group would not worship at the same place as the working class members. Fourth, in cultural activities, exclusively middle class and working class bodies existed. Fifth, trade unions stressed class solidarity. Only in political activity did some opportunity for social mixing exist, although such was not the case with all bodies.

Notes

1 See, for instance, James L. Watson, 'Introduction: Immigration, Ethnicity, and Class in Britain', in *idem* (ed.), *Between Two Cultures: Migrants and Minorities in Britain*, London, 1991 reprint, pp. 8–11; and John Rex and David Mason (eds), *Theories of Race and Ethnic Relations*, Cambridge, 1986.

2 Oscar Handlin, *The Uprooted: The Epic Story of the Great Migration that Made the American People*, London, second edition, 1979, p. 152.

3 Stephen Castles, *Here for Good: Western Europe's New Ethnic Minorities*, London, 1987, p. 96.

4 Stanley Nadel, *Little Germany: Ethnicity, Religion, and Class in New York City*, Urbana and Chicago, 1990, pp. 29–36, 48–50.

5 Kathleen Neils Conzen, 'Immigrants, Immigrant Neighborhoods, and Ethnic Identity: Historical Issues', *Journal of American History*, vol. 66, 1979, pp. 604–5.

6 Colin G. Pooley, 'The Residential Segregation of Migrant Communities in mid-Victorian Liverpool', *Transactions of the Institute of British Geographers*, vol. 2, 1977, p. 370.

7 Frank Neal, *Sectarian Violence: The Liverpool Experience, 1819–1914*, Manchester, 1988, pp. 11–15.

8 Steven Fielding, *Class and Ethnicity: Irish Catholics in England, 1880–1939*, Buckingham, 1993, pp. 28–9.

9 Mervyn A. Busteed, Robert I. Hodgson and Thomas F. Kennedy, 'The Myth and Reality of Irish Migrants in Mid-Nineteenth Century Manchester: A Preliminary Study', in P. O'Sulivan (ed.), *The Irish World Wide*, vol. 2, Leicester, 1992, pp. 34–9.

10 Lucio Sponza, *Italian Immigrants in Nineteenth Century Britain: Realities and Images*, Leicester, 1988, p. 20.

11 Handlin, *Uprooted*, p. 105.

12 Will Herberg, *Protestant–Catholic–Jew: An Essay in American Religious Sociology*, Chicago, 1983 edition, p. 14.

13 Frederick C. Luebke, *Bonds of Loyalty: German Americans and World War I*, De Kalb, Illinois, 1974, pp. 34–5.

14 Jay P. Dolan, *The Immigrant Church: New York's Irish and German Catholics, 1815–1865*, Baltimore and London, 1975, p. 58.

15 Graham Davis, *The Irish in Britain, 1815–1914*, Dublin, 1991, pp. 124–38.

16 Sheridan Gilley, 'The Roman Catholic Church and the Nineteenth-Century Irish Diaspora', *Journal of Ecclesistical History*, vol. 35, 1984, p. 195.

17 David Fitzpatrick, '"A Peculiar Tramping People": The Irish in Britain, 1801–70', in W. E. Vaughan (ed.), *A New History of Ireland*, vol. 5, Oxford, 1989, p. 651.

18 M. A. G. OTuathaigh, 'The Irish in Nineteenth Century Britain: Problems of Integration', *Transactions of the Royal Historical Society*, 5th series, vol. 31, 1981, p. 165.

19 Davis, *Irish in Britain*, p. 140.

20 Sheridan Gilley, 'The Roman Catholic Mission to the Irish in London, 1840–1860', *Recusant History*, vol. 10, 1969–70, p. 125.

21 Lynn Holden Lees, *Exiles of Erin: Irish Immigrants in Victorian London*, Manchester, 1979, p. 175.

22 *Ibid.*, p. 182.

23 *Ibid.*, p. 193.

24 Frank Boyce, 'Irish Catholicism in Liverpool between the Wars', *Labour History Review*, vol. 57, 1992, p. 20.

25 Fielding, *Class and Ethnicity*, pp. 38–78.

26 Bernard Aspinwall, 'Popery in Scotland: Image and Reality, 1820–1920', *Records of the Scottish Church History Society*, vol. 22, 1986, p. 235.

27 W. M. Walker, 'Irish Immigrants in Scotland: Their Priests, Politics and Parochial Life', *Historical Journal*, vol. 15, 1972, pp. 655–6.

28 V. D. Lipman, *Social History of the Jews in England, 1850–1980*, London, 1954, p. 45.

29 Geoffrey Alderman, *Modern British Jewry*, Oxford, 1992, pp. 142–5.

30 Henrietta Adler, 'Jewish Life and Labour in East London', in *New Survey of London Life and Labour*, vol. 6, London, 1934, pp. 276, 277.

31 Terri Colpi, *The Italian Factor: The Italian Community in Great Britain*, Edinburgh, 1991, p. 95.

32 Vared Armit Talai, *Armenians in London: The Management of Social Boundaries*, Manchester, 1989, p. 14.

33 Rozina Visram, *Ayahs, Lascars and Princes: Indians in Britain, 1700–1947*, London, 1986, p. 49.

34 OTuathaigh, 'Irish in Nineteenth Century Britain', p. 164.

35 Alderman, *Modern British Jewry*, p. 141.

36 Günther Berghaus, 'The Emigres from Nazi Germany and their Contribution to the British Theatrical Scene', in W. E. Mosse *et al.*, *Second Chance: Two Centuries of German-speaking Jews in the United Kingdom*, Tübingen 1991, pp. 299–300.

37 Charles Booth, *Life and Labour of the People in London*, first series, vol. 1, London, 1902, pp. 103–5.

38 Colpi, *Italian Factor*, p. 65.

39 John Wraight, *The Swiss in London: A History of the City Swiss Club*, London, 1991.

40 Allison Lockwood, *Passionate Pilgrims: The American Traveller in Great Britain, 1800–1914*, London, 1981, p. 15.

41 Society of American Women in London, *Constitution, By-laws, Standing Rules*, London, 1900, p. 5.

42 J. G. Colmer, *The Canada Club (London)*, London, 1934.

43 Fielding, *Class and Ethnicity*, p. 34.

44 Graham Walker, 'The Protestant Irish in Scotland', in T. M. Devine (ed.), *Irish Immigrants and Scottish Society in the Nineteenth and Twentieth Centuries*, Edinburgh, 1991, p. 51.

45 Bernard O'Connell, 'Irish Nationalism in Liverpool, 1873–1923', *Eire Ireland*, vol. 10, 1975, p. 24.

46 Geoffrey Alderman, 'The Political Impact of Zionism in the East End of London before 1940', *London Journal*, vol. 9, 1983, pp. 35–8.

47 Paul Goodman, *Zionism in England, 1899–1949*, London, 1949, p. 28.

48 *Ibid.*, p. 81.

49 Anne J. Kershen, 'Trade Unionism amongst the Jewish Tailoring Workers of London and Leeds, 1872–1915', in David Cesarani (ed.), *The Making of Modern Anglo-Jewry*, Oxford, 1990, p. 36.

50 Joseph Buckman, *Immigrants and the Class Struggle: The Jewish Immigrant in Leeds, 1880–1914*, Manchester, 1983.

51 Peter Brock, 'The Polish Revolutionary Commune in London', *Slavonic and East European Review*, vol. 35, 1956, p. 117.

52 Barry Hollingsworth, 'The Society of Friends of Russian Freedom: English Liberals and Russian Socialists, 1890–1917', *Oxford Slavonic Papers*, vol. 3, 1970, p. 51.

5

Racism

All minorities in all societies in all historical periods have endured hostility from the government and the majority populations in the countries in which they live. The differentiating factor from one example to another is the intensity and ways in which racism manifests itself. Thus the negative experience of immigrants in Britain between 1815 and 1945, however mild compared with that of minorities on the European continent in the same period, should not surprise us.

For the purposes of this chapter the concept of racism will be employed interchangeably with phrases such as anti-immigrant hostility and xenophobia. In this sense 'racism' is used in the post-1945 sociological and public opinion sense of the word, rather than in a mid-nineteenth century anthropological fashion, to distinguish different 'scientific' races of men.

Racism manifests itself in a variety of ways, which we can divide into official and unofficial. The relationship between the former and the latter is complex. While the state may be all-important in the levels and direction of racism, in some instances, particularly in liberal democracies, of which Britain is the classic example, public opinion can run ahead of the actions of the government and force it to act on particular issues, although the relationship between the two is extremely complex. We need to accept that all states are racist.

We can prove this by looking at manifestations of state xenophobia, which demonstrates itself in the following ways, nearly all of which affected Britain in the nineteenth and early twentieth centuries. Research on post-1945 Britain has especially concentrated upon the existence of an underlying racist culture in the British state, which demonstrates itself especially in the criminal justice system and the police force, which heavily discriminate against Black and Asian minorities. While similar hostility may have existed before the Second World War, it proves difficult to demonstrate its existence because of lack of evidence, although the discussion below will provide examples.

State racism also manifests itself in the introduction of legislation, especially immigration controls, already discussed, and in the passage of nationality legislation. On various occasions the British state has resorted to deportation. In more extreme circumstances, especially wartime, the state can pass measures to control the movement of enemy aliens, and even to confiscate their property. The British state has also used relocation and internment as a method of controlling minorities during the two World Wars. However, unlike in autocracies, the British government has not played a direct role in racial violence, although it has encouraged it indirectly.

Unofficial hostility towards minorities manifests itself in the following ways. In the first place, we can point to a refusal to enter into social or economic intercourse with a member of a minority, although this proves difficult to measure before 1945. More purely economic discrimination has manifested itself in a variety of ways, including refusal to employ members of a minority, and in trade union hostility, which has sometimes manifested itself in strikes. Media hostility manifests itself in two ways. First, in the existence of ever present newspaper and literary stereotypes. And, second, in the development of press campaigns over particular issues. Under conditions of intense or prolonged insecurity within a state, conspiracy theories can develop. The growth of pressure groups and political parties also indicates the development of a potent racism. Finally, racial violence can be considered the strongest form of popular racism, ranging from attacks upon individuals, which are difficult to detect in pre-1945 Britain, to riots against minorities at a particular time, involving thousands of people and systematic targeting.

All minorities in British history have endured racism. During the nineteenth and early twentieth centuries the manifestations and intensity have varied from one group to another. Factors which determine the level of hostility include the strength of underlying stereotypes, numbers, and more immediate circumstances of in- security. These include times of economic downturn, and wartime, when the most extreme hostility manifests itself.

Official racism

The rest of the discussion in this chapter will proceed along the lines of the structure outlined above, of official and unofficial racism and its various manifestations. We can begin with official racism and the first way in which it demonstrates itself in the existence of an underlying state culture as shown especially in the attitudes of the judiciary and police. Other manifestations also exist, but we need to reiterate the point previously made about the difficulties of detection.

However, we can point to the relevant research which mentions the attitudes of the judiciary and police. For instance, Roger Swift has pointed to the determination with which the police dealt with Irish crime during the mid-nineteenth century. He writes of the surveillance of working class districts which contained heavy Irish concentrations and the resentment which this caused. The Irish were more liable to arrest than the native population. Swift explains this state of affairs by asserting that police prejudice might best be explained 'in terms of a general discrimination against the "dangerous" or "criminal" sections of working-class society, within which the Irish were particularly vulnerable, rather than in terms of prejudice against the Irish *per se*, although instances of anti-Irish sentiment were undoubtedly displayed by individual policemen against Irish immigrants from time to time'.[1] Sponza has also identified police hostility towards Italians in the late nineteenth century.[2]

If we turn to the Edwardian period, an article by J. J. Tobias has superficially examined relations between the police and Jewish immigrants in the East End of London. Although the author accepts that a lack of evidence exists, he mistakenly, and evenly naively, assumes that the Edwardian years were a time of harmony between police and immigrants.[3] A clear example of prejudice in the judiciary at this time exists in the statements of Judge Rentoul, who made a speech in 1909, in which he asserted that three-quarters of the cases he tried consisted of 'aliens of the very worst type in their own country' including 'the Russian burglar, the Polish thief, the Italian stabber, and the German swindler' (see Document 25).

During the First World War, we can question whether the riots against the German community in May 1915 were adequately suppressed by the police in view of their widespread nature. Jacqueline Jenkinson has carried out detailed research into police and judicial attitudes towards the 1919 race riots against Britain's Black communities. With regard to the police she has pointed to evidence of friction with the Black communities before the Liverpool riots, as well as a tendency by the Hull, Cardiff and Glasgow police to arrest Blacks rather than Whites. The courts, however, were more equitable in their sentencing.[4] In the East End violence of the 1930s, involving fascists and, mostly Jewish, anti-fascists, the police tended to come out more heavily against the former than against the latter, according to research by D. S. Lewis and Richard Thurlow.[5]

If we turn to legislation, we see that this is a more direct way in which government racism manifests itself. Chapter 2 examined immigration Acts in some detail, and we can turn to other ways of controlling immigrants. First, nationality laws, which have been introduced against a particular minority at various times. These always exist and undergo modification because of specific circumstances. Before the First World War, the Naturalisation Act of 1870 dealt with the position of aliens. As the First World War broke out, although unconnected with it, the British Nationality and Status of Aliens Act, 1914 was making its way through Parliament. However, because of the strength of hostility towards Germans living in Britain during the First World War, the British Nationality and Status of Aliens Act, 1918 was passed. This gave the Home Secretary powers to revoke naturalisation certificates granted to Germans for a variety of reasons.

During wartime more extreme legislation comes into operation. We can again look at the First World War, when the Aliens Restriction Act came into operation, aimed at both enemy aliens and other non-British citizens. The former faced tight restrictions on a wide range of aspects of their lives, including movement, as they could not travel more than five miles from their place of residence without a permit, and could also not reside in 'prohibited areas' of strategic importance. Enemy aliens had to register with the police wherever they lived, whereas friendly ones initially only needed to do so in prohibited areas, although with the passage of time this changed to include all areas. In addition, by the end of the war all aliens had to carry identity books.

For Germans in Britain, the Aliens Restriction Act also had more wide-ranging effects, leading to the closure of German social clubs and newspapers. In addition, the government passed a series of measures, in the form of the Trading with the Enemy Acts, which led to the eradication of German business interests in Britain during the First World War, ranging in size from local bakers and pork butchers to branches of multinationals.

However, legislation is not simply a product of wartime, because at the start of the nineteenth century, numerous restrictions existed upon Jews in public life, a remnant of a pre-industrial age. These measures excluded Jews from taking part in retail trade until 1830; from practising at the bar until 1833; from holding municipal office until 1845; or from sitting in the House of Commons until 1858. Despite the passage of measures which made these developments possible, the process was slow and the struggle for Jewish emancipation faced much opposition both inside and outside Parliament, especially on the issue of sitting in the House of Commons.

On various occasions British state racism has manifested itself in deportation, sometimes in a systematic way, affecting a large proportion of a particular community. We can point to three particularly potent examples, each occurring during or shortly after a period of war. However, we should first mention the deportation of several hundred German Gypsies which took place between 1904 and 1906 against the background of intense official and public hostility at the time of the passage of the Aliens Act.

A far larger number of deportations affected the German community in Britain during the First World War. For most of the War, as we shall see below, the British government pursued a policy of interning male enemy aliens and repatriating women, but at the end of the conflict it decided to institute wholesale repatriation, which also meant the deportation of Englishwomen married to Germans who had never even visited Germany. As a result of the wholesale deportation the size of the German community during the First World War declined from 57,500 in 1914 to just 22,254 in 1919.[6]

Also in 1919 a systematic repatriation of Britain's Black communities took place in the aftermath of the riots of that year. This represented an attempt by the government 'to remove the "threat" posed by the black sailors in ports across the country'.[7] Repatriation committees were established in cities with substantial Black communities, including Hull, South Shields, Glasgow, Cardiff, Liverpool, London and Salford. These bodies had no Black representation.

The best known example of repatriation in twentieth century Britain took place during the Second World War and involved sending German and Italian prisoners of war to Australia and Canada, a decision reached in early June 1940, under prompting from the new Prime Minister, Winston Churchill. Eventually 8,000 aliens went to the Dominions.[8] One of the ships transporting prisoners of war, the *Arandora Star*, was sunk by a German submarine on 2 July, resulting in over 700 deaths,[9] and represented a turning point in the history of internment and repatriation in Britain during the Second World War, as public opinion turned against these policies.

As the above paragraphs indicate, the British government used internment as a way of controlling enemy aliens during both World Wars. In the case of the First World War the country entered the conflict without any definite policy and in the opening months of the conflict the government changed tack on numerous occasions before eventually adopting a policy of wholesale internment in May 1915 following nationwide anti-German riots that month. This remained the situation until 1919. During the course of the war over 30,000 people spent time in internment camps. The majority of these were housed on the Isle of Man in camps at Peel and, more importantly, Knockaloe. The most important camp on the mainland was Alexandra Palace in north London, which housed an average of 3,000 prisoners at any one time. The experience of internment proved difficult for some prisoners (see Document 26) even with the development of a wide range of educational and artistic activities. In addition, living conditions within the camps, especially early on, were poor.[10]

As during the First World War, in the opening months of the Second the government changed its internment policy on several occasions. Discussions in early 1939 had prepared the way for the incarceration of 18,000 prisoners. However, in the early months of the war 73,000 enemy aliens were divided into three groups by tribunals. Those in category A were regarded as suspect and a security risk and consequently faced internment; category B consisted of people who could remain at liberty but who faced some restrictions; those in group C did not face any interference. 'Of the 73,800 aliens screened, less than 1 per cent were interned and 6,200 were put into category C'.[11]

This remained the situation until the spring of 1940, by which time public opinion and the press had begun to turn against the aliens. The hostility had intensified with the rapid advance of German armies through the Low Countries and France in April and May 1940. The decision on wholesale internment was reached by the Home Defence Committee of the Cabinet on 11 June, following both Mussolini's declaration of war, and pressure from the military authorities. Therefore Chief Constables received instructions to commence immediate internment of class C aliens. In all, 22,000 Germans and Austrians and 4,300 Italians may have endured a period of internment.[12] However, by the end of July 1940, following the change in public reaction towards internment, the Home Office had already issued a White Paper which listed eighteen groups of detainees to be released. By April 1941 17,745 internees were free. At the end of August 1941 only 1,300 internees remained in camps, a figure which had fallen to just twenty five by April 1944.[13]

As in the First World War, the majority of internees found themselves in camps established on the Isle of Man. These were situated in Ramsey, Peel, Onchan, Douglas, Castletown, Port Erin and Port St Mary. The last two housed women. Fifteen camps also existed at various times on the mainland. The experience of internment resembled that of the First World War. In order to relieve the boredom and depression, internees developed artistic, literary and educational activities during their early days in internment camps.

At this point we can also mention the experience of another minority group in Britain during the Second World War, consisting of Black American GIs. Official hostility towards them was all-embracing, ranging from the level of the Cabinet and government departments to that of local police forces. In the case of the former, we can point to the fact that the Cabinet was initially reluctant to allow any Black troops to enter the country, but accepted them under pressure from the US Army. Once in the country, although welcomed to some degree by the British population, the Black GIs faced official hostility. For instance, some police forces prosecuted White women and Black soldiers who associated with each other.

Finally, we can ask whether the state has played a role in the outbreak of racial violence. Clearly, no government-led genocide took place in nineteenth and early twentieth century Britain similar to that in Australia, the United States or Germany in the same period. Nor did the police directly provoke rioters as they did in late Tsarist Russia, although we have seen that the police in Britain influenced racial outbreaks in other ways. In addition, we can also point to indirect state involvement in the anti-German riots of the First World War, especially those of May 1915, for a variety of reasons. In the first place, we can mention the fact that the disturbances took place against the background of widespread anti-German propaganda which, although not focusing directly upon the immigrants within Britain, coloured the views of the British populace towards them. At the same time, various MPs virtually encouraged the disturbances.

A preliminary assessment of state racial attitudes would point to the fact that the British government has been fundamentally racist throughout the period under consideration, whether through the introduction of legislation or in the actions of the judiciary and the police. We might argue that Britain has never had an overtly racist government of the sort that existed in Nazi Germany, but we have to balance this assertion against the fact that Britain has been a liberal democracy throughout the period under consideration, which has inevitably meant that the measures it introduced were milder. Within this context, the British state has pursued racist policies.

Unofficial racism

We may argue that because state racism in Britain has been less potent than in other states, this has allowed the development of more widespread unofficial hostility towards minorities. Unlike the situation in Nazi Germany or Tsarist Russia, it might be argued that, within Britain, public opinion influences government attitudes towards minorities to a greater extent than the state controls the actions of the populace. This appears to be the case on some occasions, but in reality the relationship between state and people in a liberal democracy is extremely complex, with the two feeding upon each other. We can proceed by examining popular racism according to the structure outlined in the introduction to this chapter.

We can begin with the refusal by a member of the dominant group to enter into social or economic intercourse with a member of the minority. We may describe this as the mildest form of racial hostility but also one of the most difficult to prove historically because of lack of evidence. However, some does exist. Bernard Gainer's comprehensive study of reactions to Jewish immigrants during the late nineteenth century examined a wide range of ways in which antisemitism manifested itself. For instance, he pointed to the hostility which Jewish costermongers faced from English street traders and shopkeepers in the East End of London owing to their perceived competition. Housing led to other forms of hostility. In the first place, natives believed that immigrant landlords put rents up. Similarly, English East Enders commented upon the fact that the newcomers had different living habits from them, focusing upon issues such as sanitary habits and food.[14]

During the First World War Germans faced the bulk of social animosity, accompanying both widespread official racism and other forms of popular hostility. Clubs and trading organisations, for instance, boycotted Germans. As early as October 1914 representatives of fifty golf clubs met at the Golfers' Club in Whitehall Court to pass a resolution, by a majority of forty nine to one, expelling German members. Stock exchanges and chambers of commerce throughout the country, including those in London, took similar action.

Much work has appeared on social antisemitism between 1919 and 1945, revealing a policy of excluding Jews by a wide variety of organisations, including a table tennis club, a motor club and a county club. Jews also faced discrimination in obtaining housing in London and Glasgow. During the Second World War Jews faced hostility in other ways. For instance, evacuation might mean the abandonment by children of Jewish rituals in order to live with a Gentile family. More generally, Jewish children faced initial hostility in the areas to which they moved. The social discrimination of the inter-war years continued. 'Clubs such as Les Ambassadeurs in Mayfair refused Jewish members as late as 1943.

Many golf clubs followed a similar policy and a numerus clausus operated in some private schools'.[15]

Blacks also faced hostility between 1919 and 1945. A survey carried out just before the outbreak of the Second World War revealed that around 40 per cent of those offering rented accommodation displayed an 'aversion' towards taking in Black tenants. Another study from 1938 demonstrated that 75 per cent of non-Whites in Liverpool were unemployed. During the Second World War discrimination in 'hotels and places of public entertainment . . . continued unabated', increasing after the arrival of Black GIs.[16] Other groups also faced discrimination during the Second World War. For instance, the businesses of some Italian shopkeepers folded because local people refused to buy goods provided by 'enemy aliens'. In a Tilbury air raid shelter meanwhile Indians faced hostility from both Gentiles and Jews.

Economic animosity has affected virtually every minority resident in Britain and has manifested itself both in the form of employers' refusal to employ members of minority groups and in trade union hostility to immigrants working in the same area of employment as their British members and supposedly threatening their conditions of employment.

Much research has been carried out on economic reactions to Jewish immigrants during the late nineteenth century. The nature of the complaints focused upon a series of particular issues, including 'the "induced" nature of much immigration', blamed primarily upon employers. More specific hostility was directed towards the view that Jews were the main causes of sweating in the trades in which they had become involved, a view shared by other sections of British society. Jews also faced resentment because of their perceived competition, caused by the fact that they worked longer hours. At the same time they were also seen as strikebreakers. Furthermore, British trade unionists believed that Jews could not combine together in unions because of their individualistic nature. Both the Trades Union Congress and specific unions opposed the immigrants. The former passed resolutions in 1888, 1889, 1890, 1892, 1893, 1894 and 1895. Although these primarily blamed the employers for importing foreign labour, some of the responsibility was clearly placed upon the immigrants themselves. However, after 1895 the TUC passed no further resolutions calling for restrictions upon immigration. Specific unions

111

which demonstrated hostility towards east European Jews were those which faced the most direct competition, including those involved in tailoring and bootmaking.

Jews faced discrimination in their attempts to secure employment. In Leeds they had to face notices declaring 'No Jews need apply'. Academics also faced antisemitism. Colin Holmes has given the example of Lewis Namier, who applied for a fellowship at All Souls College Oxford in 1911. Although he was the 'best man by far in sheer intellect . . . the Warden and majority of Fellows shied at his race', and the next two best candidates were appointed.[17]

Other groups also faced trade union hostility during the late Victorian and Edwardian years. For instance, in the Lanarkshire coalfield Lithuanian immigrants endured animosity because the union viewed them as unskilled and consequently a danger to their fellow workers. The miners also viewed the immigrants as a threat to their own employment. Chinese seamen faced hostility because of their strikebreaking activities in South Wales resulting in attacks by British and other foreign sailors upon Chinese laundries. 'The seamen's opposition to the Chinese was unremitting: it continued during the First World War and ceased only with the deportation of many Chinese seamen from Britain in 1920'.[18] We should also consider the hostility towards Chinese employees, especially on the left during the early Edwardian period, against the background of the opposition to the importation of Chinese 'coolies'. This issue actually formed one of the major planks in the Liberal party's programme for the election of 1905.

During the First World War Germans faced much economic hostility. From the opening months of the war British employers began to dismiss German staff. In October 1914, under pressure from a newspaper campaign, restaurants and hotels throughout London sacked their German waiters. In Bradford, in May 1915, the threat of an anti-German strike against twenty seven Germans employed at the Manningham Mills resulted in their dismissal. Similar events occurred in Newcastle, Sheffield, Oldham, and Ancoats in Manchester.

Immediately after the end of the First World War foreign seamen again attracted attention, one of the issues which led to the outbreak of racial violence in 1919. The problem lay in the fact that wartime demand for Black labour had ceased. Both the National Sailors' and Firemen's Union and the National Union of Ships'

Stewards, Cooks, Butchers and Bakers were 'implacably opposed to the employment of black seamen when white crews were available'.[19] Hostility to foreign seamen continued in the inter-war years, focusing upon Arabs, Somalis, West Indians and Africans. The animosity revolved around rates of pay, hiring practices and the question of British citizenship.

Jews also continued to face economic hostility after 1918, which manifested itself in various ways. Newspaper advertisements for jobs sometimes stated that no Jews should apply. Middle class German Jewish refugees from Nazism who entered the country during the 1930s faced opposition in some professions. For instance, the British Medical Association displayed strong opposition to the employment of refugees from Nazism.

Underlying the manifestations of racism outlined above, and those to be discussed below, there has always existed animosity towards immigrants in Britain in the written word. This moves us on to a complex area. The first point to recognise is that views about communities within Britain do not simply develop in a vacuum but are fundamentally influenced by the attitudes of British society towards the country of origin of the newcomers. These wider views often encompass both a positive and a negative element, although one or the other may be more dominant either throughout the period under consideration or at specific times.

The organs of the transmission of views about immigrants and their lands of origin are varied and include literature, popular novels, especially during the twentieth century, newspapers, mainstream and marginal, and racist books. From the mid-nineteenth century we can identify the development of racist ideology, in which Britain played a fundamental part, and which would touch all sections of British society with the passage of time.

As well as underlying images, especially in newspapers and books, we can also point to the fact that particular communities attract attention at specific times, during which press campaigns can develop against them. In some cases, particularly during periods of extreme insecurity, conspiracy theories can develop, which revolve around the concept of a particular immigrant group having complete control over all aspects of a particular nation's destiny. Such ideas only develop against minorities which have real or perceived power within Britain, rather than against those whose members are all at the lower end of the social scale. We can best move forward by considering individual groups in turn.

Hostility towards the Irish revolved around a series of themes. The first of these is anti-Catholicism, with traditions stretching back to the sixteenth century Reformation. 'It influenced the behaviour of all classes in English society in the nineteenth century'.[20] At the lower end of the social scale anti-Catholicism coloured the views of the English working classes in the districts where Irish immigrants settled, as 'The most virulent anti-Catholicism was to be found in the areas of substantial Irish settlement, in Lancashire and the West of Scotland'.[21] We may view anti-Cathlocism amongst the working classes as the ideological driving force which helped to give meaning to a more straightforward economic hostility caused by the competition for economic resources due to the influx of large numbers of immigrants. In addition, animosity towards Catholics received a boost from the Evangelical Revival at the start of the nineteenth century. By the 1870s it had begun to decline owing to the virtual cessation of Irish immigration.

The second major element in nineteenth century anti-Irish prejudice we can loosely describe as racial. The origins of this date back to the Middle Ages, with the concept of the Irish as primitive. Sixteenth and seventeenth century settlers in Ireland viewed the Irish as inferior in race and culture to Anglo-Saxons. During the nineteenth century this concept became more sophisticated with the development of racial ideas, although the ideology focused upon Ireland and the Irish as a whole rather than upon Irish immigrants. At the same time it had more influence upon those higher up the social scale than on the working classes. L. P. Curtis has written of 'The gradual but unmistakable transformation of Paddy, the stereotypical Irish Celt of the nineteenth century, from a drunken and relatively harmless peasant into a dangerous ape-man or simianized agitator.' He views the caricature of the ape as significant, connecting it with the publication of Darwin's theories of evolution. 'In a biological sense, Paddy had devolved, not evolved, from a primitive peasant' to 'the lowest conceivable level of the gorilla or the orangutan'. Curtis further connects this development with growing fears about the activities of Fenian bombers in Britain during the 1870s. Another element was the concern of nineteenth century historians with the origins of the English people. These scholars distinguished between Celts and Saxons.[22]

Both Sheridan Gilley and R. E. Foster have questioned Curtis's views, accusing him of simplifying the English attitude towards the Irish into one that is too negative and too purely focused upon race. Foster particularly points to the importance of class prejudice in attitudes towards the Irish, as literary images of the Irish were mainly aimed at the Victorian middle classes.[23] In defence of Curtis, he does actually make many of the above points.

If we turn to antisemitism in Britain, we find that it has a history as old as that of anti-Irish prejudice, as well as a complexity covering religion, class, politics and race, with variations upon particular focuses over time. The organs of the transmission of antisemitic ideas cover all types of publications, as well as manifesting themselves on all levels from literary images to conspiracy theories. Although always present in British society, antisemitism has reached peaks at particular times, especially in the late nineteenth and early twentieth centuries.

We can proceed chronologically, focusing upon the period until the 1870s. We can begin with William Cobbett, the populist agitator for parliamentary reform, who we may see as a forerunner of a tradition of left-wing antisemitism. In a publication of 1830, entitled *Good Friday or the Murder of Jesus Christ by the Jews*, Cobbett launches a violent attack upon Jews as moneylenders (see Document 27).

Similar themes arise in antisemitism in nineteenth century literature. One of the standard works on this theme points to the importance of a Jewish character's financial position. 'Good or bad, rich Jews or poor, tyrant or slave, money was almost bound to be at the root of his problem'.[24] Among the major nineteenth century Jewish figures we can point to Isaac in Walter Scott's *Ivanhoe*, who has some positive points, and Fagin, in *Oliver Twist*, whose portrayal is almost completely negative. Anthony Trollope's Jews vary from those portrayed neutrally to Melmotte, in *The Way We Live Now*, who is viewed as a corrupting influence in English society. We can also point to George du Maurier's 'ludicrously sinister Jew, Svengali'.[25] In periodical literature the image of the Jew during the nineteenth century was not all negative. *Punch*, for instance, whilst it carried cartoons of Jews 'as foreign types, with black, curly hair, enormous noses, thick bulbous lips',[26] also supported the campaign for Jewish emancipation in the early part of the century.

In the late Victorian and Edwardian years antisemitism, in

common with developments in other parts of Europe, became a major political issue in Britain. It took on various forms, focusing upon a range of issues from the question of the immigration of poor Jews in eastern Europe to the perceived threat of rich Jews and their influence in British society and politics, a question which affected both the left and right of the political spectrum. The growth of antisemitism was also assisted by the spread of racial ideas from the mid-nineteenth century.

Hostility towards poor east European Jews moving into Britain began to take off significantly during the 1880s, manifesting itself in the production of a series of official reports, as well as in the development of a press campaign, which eventually led to the passage of the Aliens Act of 1905. J. A. Garrard has summarised the anti-alien attitude as follows: 'England was being subjected each year to an invasion by thousands, or even hundreds of thousands, of aliens, made the more serious by the growing uniqueness of England's outdatedly sentimental policy of keeping open house to all comers, and one which might, at any moment, reach catastrophic proportions should Russo-Jewish emigration develop into a general exodus'.[27] The hostility towards the newcomers focused upon particular issues. Embracing all other questions, we can point to the idea of east European Jews as distinct from British society, and likely to remain so for several generations (see Document 28). The newcomers were also seen as unhealthy and insanitary, as well as in competition for jobs and housing in the areas where they settled. Futhermore, Jews, together with other minorities in the campaign for the Aliens Act of 1905, also faced hostility because of their perceived criminality. After 1905, public opinion's concentration upon poor Jewish immigrants lessened.

Hostility towards the influence of rich Jews did not lessen and, in fact, reached one of several peaks after 1910. By this time, we can actually speak of a theory of a Jewish conspiracy circulating in England, claiming that wealthy Jews controlled various aspects of the British establishment. This affected both left and right, as mentioned. The former, in fact, experienced one major peak of antisemitism during the Boer War. A pamphlet, signed by eighty three executive officers of trade unions, claimed that 'The capitalists who brought up or hire the Press both in South Africa and in England to clamour for War are largely Jews and foreigners'.[28] J. A. Hobson, the liberal journalist, played a major role in propagating similar ideas. He claimed that the economic resources of the Transvaal had fallen 'into the hands of a small group of international financiers, chiefly German in origin and Jewish in race', who would establish 'an oligarchy of German Jews at Pretoria'. He further claimed that 'We are fighting to place a small international oligarchy of mine owners and speculators in power at Pretoria'.[29]

Anti-semitism on the right of the political spectrum can be linked with the growth of a radical right-wing ideology connected with the relative decline of Britain in the years leading up to the First World War. Those who adhered to such views partly blamed Jews for the country's decline. We can, for instance, point to Leopold Maxse, the editor of the *National Review*, who asserted that Britain was under the control of German Jews working with the Liberal government and the press. Antisemitism reached a peak in the years 1912–13 in connection with the Marconi scandal. However, hostility towards rich Jews existed throughout the late Victorian and Edwardian years. Other prominent racists included Joseph Banister, who engaged in 'a particularly savage brand of antisemitic hostility', obsessed with the conspiratorial idea of Jews dominating British society,[30] although he attacked Jews on all points on the social scale (see Document 29). We can make similar assertions about the journalist Arnold White (see Document 30). The main literary antisemite in early twentieth century Britain was Hilaire Belloc, who created the character of I. Z. Barnett, a socially mobile German-Jewish financier.

Antisemitic ideology continued to manifest itself during the course of the First World War, usually combining with hostility towards Germany, and consequently focusing upon rich Jews of German origin. Individual financiers faced attack in the press, including Sir Edgar Speyer and Sir Ernest Cassel. Conspiracy theories about German control of Britain also developed, some of them stressing inextricable links between Jews and Germany, most notably put forward by J. H. Clarke, in his *England under the Heel of the Jew*, which appeared in 1917.

Antisemitic conspiracy theories continued in the immediate aftermath of the Great War. The theme changed from linking Jews with Germans to connecting Jews with Bolsheviks and blaming them for the Russian Revolution and the spread of Communism generally. Both the *Morning Post* and *The Times* gave varying degrees of support to such ideas, especially after the publication of the

English translation of 'the notorious tasrist forgery' *The Protocols of the Elders of Zion*, in February 1920, which claimed that 'a Jewish conspiracy was planning to take over the world'.[31] Ideas about an antisemitic conspiracy continued to circulate during the inter-war years, propagated especially by extremist organisations such as the Britons and the British Union of Fascists. In addition, Fleet Street continued to put forward milder forms of antisemitism, expressing hostility, for instance, to the entry of refugees from Nazism.

Attitudes towards Germans in Britain between 1815 and 1945 have been extremely complex. For much of the nineteenth century there existed an underlying positive image of Germany, which focused upon the beauty of the countryside, the educational, philosophical and musical achievements of the country, and the racial affinity between the two nations. In contrast, another underlying image of Germans stressed their perceived uncouthness (see Document 31). German immigrants in nineteenth century Britain faced three different types of hostility. First, that based upon social prejudice, which asserted that the newcomers were immoral and drunken. Germans also experienced some of the opposition experienced by foreign musicians during the mid-nineteenth century. The second strand of hostility towards German immigrants focused upon their economic threat, especially in the trades where they were employed in large numbers such as clerical work and waiting. However, the bulk of the animosity towards Germans was politically based and originated in the fact that Germany threatened Britain's world position during the Edwardian years. This led to accusations about all Germans in Britain serving as spies, a view put forward both in the press and in popular novels.

'Spy fever' took off to a far greater extent during the First World War, especially during the opening of the conflict. However, as time passed a sophisticated conspiracy theory developed asserting that Germans controlled all sections of the British establishment and were therefore preventing victory in the war. By 1918 such ideas had become extravagant, mixed with claims that German spies had sexually corrupted Britain.

British attitudes towards Italians were as complex as views of Germany. Once again we can point to a positive image of the Italian countryside, and a negative one of the Italian people who lived in it. In addition, hostility also existed to Catholicism within the country. During the nineteenth century, basically hostile attitudes developed towards Italian immigrants in Britain, in which class prejudice played a fundamental role. A series of press campaigns developed. The most intense occurred in the 1850s and 1860s against Italian, and other immigrant, street musicians and led to the passage of the Street Music (Metropolis) Act, to control them. Later during the Victorian and Edwardian years press campaigns also developed which focused upon the perceived insanitary living and working conditions of Italians, as well as upon their supposed criminal activities. The major twentieth century peak of press hostility towards Italians occurred in the spring of 1940, following Mussolini's declaration of war on Britain.

When we move on to attitudes towards non-European groups, we are dealing with views which we can comfortably describe as racist in a nineteenth century pseudo-scientific and ideological sense of the word. Part of the reason for negative attitudes towards Blacks and Asians lay in European contact with new parts of the world. In addition, these views were also affected by events on the international scene such as the Indian Mutiny of 1857, the American Civil War, and the Jamaican revolt of 1865. Travel books published about Africa and Asia reveal overwhelmingly negative images (see Document 32). Victorians disliked the physical appearance of Black skin and further found the nakedness of Africans repulsive. In addition, they saw Blacks as lazy, superstitious, dishonest and sexually promiscuous. Negative attitudes towards Indians focused upon religion, the treatment of women, the caste system, and the Indian temperament.

However, from the mid-nineteenth century, attitudes towards non-Whites became influenced by the growing interest in racial questions in which organisations such as the English Ethnological Society and the Anthropological Society of London played a leading role. Michael Banton has spoken of mid-Victorian racial thought as a social construction, in which Europeans, who had passed through the industrialisation process, 'unconsciously imposed their social categories upon other peoples'.[32] Prominent mid-Victorian racial thinkers included Robert Knox, who regarded the 'dark races of men' as 'generally inferior to the Saxon and the Celt', claiming that brains and skulls differed, and that they would never become 'civilised'.[33] James Hunt and John Crawford (see Document 33), prominent mid-Victorian anthropologists, produced publications which distinguished the physical characteristics of Africans from other races of men.

Such views remained into the twentieth century. In an article on imperial fiction in late Victorian and Edwardian Britain Frances Mannsaker has examined images of natives. She points to the fact that a categorisation of natives existed in this form of literature ranging from, at the top, 'high caste gentlemen' to, at the bottom, 'savages' who were 'frequently cruel and violent' and whose 'constant quality is animal-like, they are to a greater or lesser extent sub-human'.[34] Clearly, views of Africans and Asians in their homeland influenced attitudes towards these groups in Britain.

British views of the Chinese were mostly negative, although some admiration of Chinese art existed during the nineteenth century. But attitudes towards the Chinese state were negative. In addition, in racial hierarchies the Chinese came fairly low down the scale. Furthermore, we can point to negative literary images of the Chinese, most notably in the work of Sax Rohmer, who created the villain Fu Manchu. Hostility towards Chinese immigrants in Britain reached something of a peak during the first two decades of the twentieth century. Issues which received particular attention included the perceived threats of Chinese labour and the opium smoking activities of immigrants, together with their marrying of English women and their living conditions. The instruments which transmitted such views included local and national newspapers, as well as books.

This brief survey of literary attitudes towards immigrants in Britain serves as an introduction to the complexity of issues involved. An examination of pressure groups and political parties reveals a more straightforward picture. Virtually every major flow of immigration to Britain has resulted in the development of organisations to oppose it. These have usually remained pressure groups of varying sizes, although they have sometimes developed into full-blown political parties, which, however, have had little electoral impact.

During the course of the nineteenth century numerous anti-Catholic bodies developed within Britain, inspired partly by the Irish influx. The previous chapter mentioned the most important of these in the form of Orange Orders, the bulk of whose membership consisted of Protestant Irish immigrants. In addition, John Wolffe has pointed to the existence of numerous other anti-Catholic bodies in nineteenth century Britain. These varied from the British (Protestant) Reformation Society, established in 1827, to the North of England Protestant Organisation, set up in 1855, although many of the groups had limited support.

The Jewish influx of the late nineteenth century led to the foundation of new anti-alien organisations based in the East End of London. The first of these, the Society for the Suppression of the Immigration of Destitute Aliens, was founded in 1886 and financed by Arnold White and the Earl of Dunraven, but it had no impact. Neither did the Association for Preventing the Immigration of Destitute Aliens. The most important East End grouping was the British Brothers' League, established in 1901 under the leadership of the Conservative MP for Stepney, Major William Evans-Gordon. This organisation aimed at preventing the movement into Britain of poor immigrants. At one stage the British Brothers' League claimed to have 45,000 members, although this is almost certainly an exaggeration.[35] In 1904 meetings took place in its support in Leicester, Bedford and Kettering. Although it remained a pressure group, it received support from Conservative MPs. A final anti-alien group which came into existence was the Immigration Reform Association, established in 1903.

During the First World War numerous anti-German organisations were founded. The most important of these was the British Empire Union, which aimed at 'the Extirpation – Root and Branch and Seed – of German Control and Influence from the British Empire'. By 1918 it may have had 10,000 members.[36] Smaller pressure groups included the Anti-German League, the League of Londoners, and the Britain for the British Movement. More important were the Vigilantes and the National Party, both of which were parliamentary parties with a small number of MPs and a radical right-wing agenda, of which Germanophobia represented just one element.

In the inter-war years antisemitism replaced hostility towards Germans as the main driving force of racist pressure groups, of which a large number developed. The Britons came into existence in 1918, with Henry Hamilton Beamish as president. The organisation restricted membership to people of British birth. In their publications the Britons made clear their obsession with the idea of a world Jewish conspiracy and the threat of Bolshevism. An article in their journal in 1924 suggested that the only solution to the Jewish problem lay either in the extermination or in the expulsion of British Jews. 'More resembling a club than a political party, the Britons never succeeded in recruiting a mass membership'. In fact, they never seem to have counted more than 100 members.[37]

In 1928 the Imperial Fascist League (IFL) came into existence, with Arnold Leese becoming its leader in 1930. Richard Thurlow has written that 'Leese's virulent antisemitism and racial fascist beliefs made him equivalent in outlook to an English Hitler'.[38] Like the Britons, the IFL preached extreme antisemitism, putting forward similarly radical solutions of either killing, sterilising or segregating Jews. Also like the Britons, the IFL remained small, never attracting more than a few hundred members.[39]

The British Union of Fascists (BUF) was the most substantial extreme right-wing group which existed in inter-war Britain. This full-blown party was founded in October 1932 by Sir Oswald Mosley, who had moved to this part of the political spectrum via the Unionists, Liberals, Labour and the New Party, which he had established in 1931. Initially, the BUF was generally anti-alien, but by the end of 1933 it had become strongly antisemitic, with its newspaper, *Blackshirt*, constantly putting antisemitism forward in terms of conspiracy theory (see Document 34). In addition, the party also carried out its main activities in the East End of London, involving the intimidation of the local Jewish population through the holding of meetings as well as physical attacks. The BUF was by far the largest fascist group in inter-war Britain, reaching a possible peak membership of 50,000 in February 1934.[40] However, it involved itself in little persistent activity outside the East End. The organisation suffered a fatal blow with the outbreak of the Second World War and the internment of its leaders in 1940.

In addition to the above three major inter-war groupings smaller ones existed, including the British Fascists and the National Socialist League. However, significantly, in contrast especially to Germany, no extreme grouping has ever seized power in Britain. The reasons for this are complex, but of fundamental importance are the long-term stable political traditions of Britain, with an unwritten constitution dating back to the seventeenth century, which mean that a short-term political or economic crisis is unlikely to shake the solidity of those foundations, in contrast to Germany,

122

where the newly established and unpopular Weimar constitution of 1919 could be blown away by the economic catastrophe of the late 1920s and early 1930s.

Before reaching a conclusion, we can briefly outline the history of the most potent form of animosity in modern Britain in the form of racial violence. The manifestations of this vary from attacks involving a few individuals upon one person or one property to full scale nationwide rioting involving tens of thousands of people throughout the country attacking thousands of shops. Attacks upon individuals are constant in British history but it proves difficult to measure them, and research still remains to be carried out on this subject.

During the course of the nineteenth century racial violence involving English natives and Irish immigrants was almost endemic in relations between the two groups, especially in Liverpool. However, violence occurred elsewhere, even in rural areas, where railway navvies and agricultural labourers endured hostility. In other cases riots took place against the Irish, notably in Stockport in June 1852. But in most instances, we are essentially referring to communal violence in which the Irish either retaliated or initiated disturbances, a process which was possible due to their numerical strength.

In Edwardian Britain Russian Jewish and Chinese immigrants faced attack. The former became the victims of small scale incidents in the areas in which they settled in large numbers, including the East End of London and the Leylands area of Leeds. The only major disturbances in Edwardian Britain occurred in South Wales in 1911, an area in which the Chinese also faced attack during the same year. The reasons for these developments lie not in any potent tradition of racism in the area, but in the local economic situation.

The two most widespread instances of racial violence occurred within a few years of each other in 1915 against the German communities of Britain and in 1919 when Britain's Black population became the victims. Anti-German riots also broke out during the first year of the Great War, affecting east London and Keighley in August 1914, and south London and Crewe during October. However, the most widespread riots in modern British history occurred in May 1915, affecting every part of Britain, from north to south and east to west. The worst violence occurred in major cities, including Manchester, Liverpool, Sheffield and, particularly,

London (see Document 35), where 2,000 properties suffered damage at a cost of £200,000. But German shops had their windows smashed virtually everywhere, including towns such as Castleford, Bury St Edmunds, Greenock, Goldthorpe and Walton-on-Thames. Further minor outbreaks of anti-German violence occurred in London in June 1916 and July 1917.

Against the intolerant background of the First World War, other groups also endured violence, including pacifists and members of other minorities, notably Russian Jews in Leeds in June 1917 (see Document 36) and east London in September the same year, sparked off in both cases by the unfounded perception of the native population that Russian Jews were avoiding military service.

The 1919 riots occurred against the background of post-war dislocation, especially, as we have seen, in the shipping industry, where Blacks and Whites competed for jobs. Nine major locations experienced disorder between January and August: Glasgow, South Shields, Salford, London, Hull, Liverpool, Cardiff, Newport and Barry. In contrast with the 1915 anti-German riots, attacks occurred to a greater extent against individuals so that at least three Black people were murdered.

During the inter-war years no large scale race riots occurred in Britain. However, as we have seen, small scale attacks broke out against Jews in east London, involving the BUF as agitators. Finally, in our period, Italians faced attack in June 1940, following Mussolini's declaration of war. The riots affected several parts of the country, notably London, Liverpool, the north-east, South Wales and Scotland, but they remained minor in comparison with the events of May 1915.

Conclusion

Clearly, all minorities in modern British history have endured racism in its various manifestations. In this sense there can be no doubt, as with virtually all human societies, that Britain is a racist country. We can see British racism as a classic example of animosity in the classic liberal democracy. We should not look for examples of hostility to immigrants and minorities becoming the main reason for the existence of the state. The essence of liberal democracy is that it is a subtle form of government, in which sudden changes rarely occur. Full scale repression and intolerance are not part of such a system. Instead, what we need to look for are less extreme manifestations of social and political activity, including examples of racism. Therefore, within the context of a liberal democracy, anti-immigrant hostility manifests itself in the way we would expect. For instance, the state has used legislation, particularly in the form of immigration controls. It has not exterminated its minorities in wartime, but has interned them. Public opinion has played a greater role in the formation of racial policies than it could do in an autocracy.

Can we view racism in British society as constant, or does it reach peaks at particular times? If so, why? Furthermore, have some minorities fared worse than others? We can give a positive answer to both parts of the first question. Some manifestations of racism are constant, such as underlying literary images and small scale physical attacks. However, there are occasions when racism reaches a peak, usually against particular minorities. We can point to the Irish in the mid-nineteenth century, Russian Jews in the late Victorian and Edwardian years, Germans during the First World War, Jews in the inter-war years, and enemy aliens in World War II. Do any factors connect these periods together?

In the first place, we can point to the impact of a sudden influx of immigrants, with regard to both the Irish and the Russian Jews, who competed for resources with the local working classes. War is also important, as intolerance always increases. The explanation for the hostility of the 1930s lies in the position of the British economy. However, in all cases we have to point to the previous existence of traditions of anti-German feeling, antisemitism and Germanophobia, which the medium term crises brought to the surface. Absolute peaks of racism occurred after particular incidents such as Mussolini's declaration of war on Britain in June 1940.

Notes

1 Roger Swift, 'Crime and the Irish in Nineteenth Century Britain', in Roger Swift and Sheridan Gilley (eds), *The Irish in Britain, 1815–1939*, London, 1989, p. 178.

2 Lucio Sponza, *Italian Immigrants in Nineteenth Century Britain: Realities and Images*, Leicester, 1988, p. 241.

3 J. J. Tobias, 'Police–Immigrant Relations in England: 1880–1910', *New Community*, vol. 3, 1974, pp. 211–14.

4 Jacqueline Jenkinson, 'The 1919 Riots', in Panikos Panayi (ed.), *Racial Violence in Britain, 1840–1950*, Leicester, 1993, pp. 98–102.

5 D. S. Lewis, *Illusions of Grandeur: Mosley, Fascism and British Society, 1931–81*, Manchester, 1987, p. 166; Richard Thurlow, 'Blaming the Blackshirts: The Authorities and the Anti-Jewish Disturbances of the 1930s', in Panayi, *Racial Violence*, p. 120.

6 Panikos Panayi, *The Enemy in our Midst: Germans in Britain during the First World War*, Oxford, 1991, p. 97.

7 Jenkinson, '1919 Riots', p. 103.

8 Bernard Wasserstein, *Britain and the Jews of Europe, 1939–1945*, Oxford, 1988, p. 96.

9 Terri Colpi, *The Italian Factor: The Italian Community in Great Britain*, Edinburgh, 1991, p. 115.

10 Panayi, *Enemy in our Midst*, chapter 3.

11 Michael Seyfert, '"His Majesty's Most Loyal Internees": The Internment and Deportation of German and Austrian Refugees as "Enemy Aliens"', in Gerhard Hirschfeld (ed.), *Exile in Great Britain: Refugees from Hitler's Germany*, Leamington Spa, 1984, p. 166.

12 Colin Holmes, '"British Justice at Work": Internment in the Second World War', in Panikos Panayi (ed.), *Minorities in Wartime: National and Racial Groupings in Britain, North America and Australia during the Two World Wars*, Oxford, 1993, p. 151.

13 Wasserstein, *Britain and the Jews of Europe*, pp. 107–8.

14 Bernard Gainer, *The Alien Invasion: The Origins of the Aliens Act of 1905*, London, 1972, pp. 31–52.

15 Tony Kushner, *The Persistence of Prejudice: Antisemitism in British Society during the Second World War*, Manchester, 1989, p. 96.

16 John Flint, 'Scandal at the Bristol Hotel: Some Thoughts on Racial Discrimination in Britain and West Africa and its Relationship to the Planning of Decolonisation, 1939–47', *Journal of Imperial and Commonwealth History*, vol. 12, 1983, pp. 76–7.

17 Colin Holmes, *Anti-Semitism in British Society, 1876–1939*, London, 1979, p. 110.

18 J. P. May, 'The Chinese in Britain, 1860–1914', in Colin Holmes (ed.), *Immigrants and Minorities in British Society*, London, 1978, p. 116.

19 Peter Fryer, *Staying Power: The History of Black People in Britain*, London, 1984, p. 298.

20 E. R. Norman, *Anti-Catholicism in Victorian England*, London, 1968, p. 16.

21 John Wolffe, *The Protestant Crusade in Great Britain 1829–1860*, Oxford, 1991, p. 2.

22 L. P. Curtis, *Apes and Angels: The Irishman in Victorian Caricature*, Newton Abbot, 1971; *idem, Anglo-Saxons and Celts*, New York, 1968.

23 Sheridan Gilley, 'English Attitudes to the Irish in England, 1780–1900', in Holmes, *Immigrants and Minorities*, pp. 81–110; R. F. Foster, 'Paddy and Mr Punch', *Journal of Newspaper and Periodical History*, vol. 7, 1991, pp. 33–47.

24 Edgar Rosenberg, *From Shylock to Svengali: Jewish Stereotypes in English Fiction*, Stanford, California, 1960, p. 262.

25 Pauline Paucker, 'The Image of the German Jews in English Fiction', in W. E. Mosse *et al.* (ed.), *Second Chance: Two Centuries of German-speaking Jews in the United Kingdom*, Tübingen, 1991, p. 321.

26 Beatrice Rosenblum, '*Punch* and the Jews, 1841–1858', *Transactions of the Jewish Historical Society of England*, vol. 24, 1970–3, p. 206.

27 John A. Garrard, *The English and Immigration, 1880–1910*, Oxford, 1971, pp. 51–2.

28 John S. Galbraith, 'The Pamphlet Campaign in the Boer War', *Journal of Modern History*, vol. 24, 1952, pp. 120–1.

29 J. A. Hobson, *The War in South Africa: Its Causes and Effects*, London, 1900, pp. 189, 196, 197.

30 Holmes, *Anti-Semitism*, p. 39.

31 Sharman Kadish, '"Boche, Bolshie and the Jewish Bogey": The Russian Revolution and Press Antisemitism in Britain, 1917–21', *Patterns of Prejudice*, vol. 22, 1988, p. 30.

32 Michael Banton, *The Idea of Race*, London, 1977, p. 13.

33 Robert Knox, *The Races of Men*, London, 1862, pp. 226, 244.

34 Frances M. Mannsaker, 'The Dog that didn't Bark: The Subject Races in Imperial Fiction at the Turn of the Century', in David Dabydeen (ed.), *The Black Presence in English Literature*, Manchester, 1985, p. 119.

35 Christopher T. Husbands, 'East End Racism, 1900–1980: Geographical Continuities in Vigilante and Extreme Right-wing Political Behaviour', *London Journal*, vol. 8, 1982, p. 7.

36 Panayi, *Enemy in our Midst*, pp. 203–7.

37 Gisela C. Lebzelter, *Political Anti-Semitism in England, 1918–1939*, New York, 1978, pp. 65–6.

38 Richard Thurlow, *Fascism in Britain: A History, 1918–1985*, Oxford, 1987, p. 71.

39 Lebzelter, *Political Anti-Semitism*, p. 83.

40 Thurlow, *Fascism in Britain*, p. 122.

Conclusion

Any history of Britain during the nineteenth and twentieth centuries cannot ignore the experience of minorities. They form a fundamental strand in the the development of the country since 1815. Their experience remains as important as that of the working classes and of women. The only difference is the fact that immigrants and their offspring have involved smaller numbers than these two groups.

Newcomers represent a strand of British society that is fundamentally part of it and distinct from it. With regard to the immigration process this can be understood, from a non-British point of view, by examining push factors which led people to leave the land of their birth. However, they could only have entered the country because the British economy allowed them to do so. The structure of the immigrant communities and their ethnicity is also both part of and distinct from British society. Newcomers may live in their own communities in the first generation but their social structure is fundamentally tied to the British class system. They cannot escape from this. Within their own communities, class plays a fundamental role. Ethnicity may simply seem a way in which minorities differentiate themselves from British society, but we should also recognise that the nature of ethnicity mirrors the religious, social and cultural activities of the various native classes in Britain.

How does the experience of minorites in Britain between 1815 and 1945 compare with that of similar groupings in other parts of the world? We can make particular comparisons with the United

States and Germany, as well as with other states. With regard to immigration, Britain closely resembles Germany in the sense that, while it may have seen an influx of millions of people during these years, both states have also suffered a large population loss. In the case of Britain this has been almost purely due to the economic opportunities available in North America and Australia, while Germany has exported people owing to its less advanced economy during the nineteenth century and owing to political persecution, especially under the Nazis. The United States differs from both Germany and Britain in the sense that it has simply been a country of immigration from 1815 to 1945. The numbers of newcomers entering the country also differ, with the United States having far greater pulling power than either Britain or Germany.

However, we can draw parallels with regard to immigration in all three. The most fundamental similarity is the fact that for most of the period under consideration, they were the leading industrial nations, providing economic opportunities which attracted immigrants from similar places of origin, particularly Italy and Russia, although we can identify differences in other cases. The periods of greatest immigration are similar between Britain and the United States in the sense that both countries had a virtually open door policy, which began to change in the late nineteenth century, so that by the inter-war years both had imposed strict controls upon entry under the impact of economic recession.

The structure of immigrant groupings demonstrates both parallels and similarites within the three countries. With regard to geographical concentration, there was not the focus upon New York or Berlin, that there was upon London. In the United States, while New York represented a major centre, large concentrations of immigrants lived in other major north-eastern and mid-western cities. At the same time, some newcomers did not settle in an urban environment, but took up farming in the mid-west, a pattern whose only parallel in Britain is Irish agricultural labourers, who, however, certainly did not purchase farms. In Germany a similar development occurred at the end of the nineteenth century with the importation of Polish agricultural labourers into East Prussia.

Family structure could best develop in the United States because of larger numbers of immigrants involved, although this is not the entire picture because some groups, such as Italians, consisted,

129

to a great degree, of males. Employment structure was varied in both the United States and Britain, with concentration in similar employments. Construction, mining and steel making proved particularly important in Germany, especially in the Ruhr during the late nineteenth century. Social hierarchies varied from one group to another. In both Germany and Britain, we can point to an established Jewry fearing the immigration of poor east European Jews at the end of the nineteenth century, while in both the United States and Britain, Germans has a well developed class structure.

Ethnicity could develop to a greater extent in the United States than in Britain because of the size of the communities involved. Ethnic neighbourhoods in US cities were common for many of the European communities. Size played a role in the availability of marriage partners from the same group. We can also make comparisons with Tsarist Russia here, where ethnicity amongst Jews was extremely solid, owing, in large measure, to state persecution, which did not allow movement outside Jewry. Such factors operated to a lesser extent in the United States and Britain.

Ethnic organisations developed in all three countries amongst established urban communities, based on religion, culture and politics. The last of these played a smaller role in Germany because the autocratic nature of the state meant that refugees were unlikely to move there. Class differences proved important in the development of ethnic groupings amongst the larger minorities, as the case of Germans in London and New York reveals.

If we move into the field of racism within the three countries, into which we can also bring other examples, we can discover fundamental differences. We can begin with the role of the state. In Nazi Germany, as in Tsarist Russia, the state fundamentally led racism, as it did in the United States with regard to Blacks, both before and after the abolition of slavery, although with regard to European groups its role was far less crude. In fact, it resembled Britain, where, as we have seen, the state was often influenced by public opinion. But overall, in comparison with most major industrialised nations, the British government role has been less important. In Germany, Russia, the United States and Australia, state-led racial violence against specific minorities has occurred, whereas in Britain we cannot find straightforward examples of such policies, partly because of the liberal state which existed in Britain but also owing to the fact that race has been less of an *internal* political issue in Britain than it has been in any of the above countries.

Nevertheless, all the Anglo-Saxon countries viewed themselves as racially superior to other states and cultures with the development of pseudo-scientific racism from the mid-nineteenth century. Within the ideas that circulated a hierarchy was created in which Anglo-Saxons formed the peak of the pyramid, underneath which came all other races, including Celts, Jews, Orientals and Africans.

It proves difficult to reach overall conclusions about the experience of minorities in the three major industrialised states between 1815 and 1945. All have witnessed significant inflows of population, although both Britain and Germany have suffered large losses of people. Structure of communities and ethnicity has varied from country to country and from one group to another. Each of the three states has been racist but the manifestations of racism and its intensity have varied from one to the other.

We can also draw comparisons in the situation of minorities in Britain before and after 1945. Academic and popular thinking has recognised the fact that immigrants have had a profound impact upon British society since the war and consequently enormous media and scholarly attention has focused upon them, allowing us to draw parallels with the situation before 1945.

If we begin with immigration, a first observation we can make concerns the fact that pull factors have played a far more significant role than they did before the war. In the case of virtually all the major inflows a recruitment process has taken place involving the state and industry. This particularly applies to the entry into the country of all groups until 1962, when the Commonwealth Immigrants Act was passed. In the immediate post-war years Britain endured a labour shortage and consequently recruited manpower from wherever it was available, first in Europe and then from its colonies. However, once the labour shortage ended, immigration controls went up to gradually reduce the types of people who could enter Britain. We can view this as a process which has developed during the whole course of the nineteenth and twentieth centuries, so that since the Aliens Act of 1905 the opportunities for entry into Britain have been constantly reduced, to the extent that we now virtually live in 'Fortress Britain'. Even refugees have difficulty moving to Britain, in comparison with other European states, especially Sweden and Germany, but again this is the continuation of a tradition of limiting political exiles which began in the 1920s. Entry into Britain has now been restricted to racially and economically safe newcomers, notably White Commonwealth immigrants and European Community nationals.

With regard to the structure of newcomers, there have also been changes since the war. Although some concentration focuses upon London, settlement has become far more widespread, resembling only the nineteenth century Irish and, to a lesser extent, pre-1945 Jewish settlement. While all Asian groupings are concentrated in particular parts of London, important clusters also exist in, for instance, Bradford, for Pakistanis, and Leicester for Sikhs and East African Asians. West Indians can be found in significant numbers in parts of Birmingham, Liverpool, Manchester and Nottingham. In other cases London proves fundamental, especially for Greek Cypriots, heavily concentrated in particular areas in the north of the capital. Gender structure varies from one group to another, so that among Greek Cypriots the sexes are almost equally represented, while Pakistanis tended initially to consist predominantly of males.

Social and employment structure varies from group to group, again resembling the pre-1945 situation. Greek Cypriots have representatives in all classes, varying from millionaires to members of the underclass. If we took Asian groups as a whole we could make similar observations, although different groups have different social concentrations. For West Indians, there exists a greater focus among the lower classes, so that the most deprived group in contemporary British society is unquestionably working, or underclass, Black youth, who have to face both social and racial prejudice.

Ethnicity has developed to at least as great an extent as it did in the pre-1945 period. Ethnic neighbourhoods characteristic of nineteenth century US cities exist for all minorities. In Leicester, for instance we can point to the fact that different groups of Asians live off particular streets in various parts of Highfields and Evington in the inner city, while Oadby is the area of settlement for the Asian bourgeoisie. Classic ethnic neighbourhoods exist amongst Greek Cypriots in London, in the mostly working class community in Green Lanes, Harringay off which countless roads are inhabited by immigrants. A higher social class lives in Palmers Green, again concentrated in particular streets, while the wealthiest

Conclusion

Greek Cypriots have moved to the more prosperous areas of north London in Southgate, Cockfosters and Finchley. Whilst intermarriage with natives takes place to some extent amongst all immigrant minorities, especially those of European origin, marriages between members of the same group, often arranged, continue into the second generation.

Ethnic organisations have developed for all groups. Italians, Poles and Irish pray in Catholic churches, West Indians join a variety of denominations, Greek Cypriots attend their Greek Orthodox churches, while Asians pray in their mosques and temples. Cultural activities are as all-embracing as those before 1945, with more of an emphasis on sport than before. For political refugees, continuing their struggle also proves important.

Has the nature of racism changed since the war? In some ways it has become controlled and less potent. The state has acted positively with the passage of race relations legislation which attempts to prevent discrimination. The media have recognised that Britain is a multicultural society and present some positive images of Blacks and Asians. People of Asian origin have become some of the most successful businessmen in Britain.

However, Britain remains a racist country. The state strictly controls the racial make-up of those whom it allows to enter 'Fortress Britain', and deportation is regularly used against those who enter the country illegally. Anti-Black racism is endemic in the judiciary, the police and the education system. Nationality legislation discriminates upon racial grounds.

Public opinion is fundamentally racist. While some positive media stereotypes may exist, so do negative ones, especially in the right-wing popular press. However, since the 1950s there has been a decline in the refusal to enter into social and economic intercourse with members of a minority group, while trade union hostility has lessened. However, racist pressure groups and political parties have always existed since the Second World War, reaching a peak of support during the 1970s. At the same time, while large scale anti-immigrant riots may have lessened, murderous racial attacks have replaced them.

In short, there are both continuities and new developments in the history of immigrant minorities in Britain before and after 1945. Because of the more complete documentation after 1945, we can form a fuller picture of the contemporary situation. However, we

133

can make the following assertions for the whole course of the nineteenth and twentieth centuries. First, Britain has witnessed, for a complex of reasons, the constant entry of a wide variety of immigrants, who have played an important role in the development of the economy. Second, these groups have varied in size, social composition, and gender make-up, but they are part of British capitalist class society, not distinct from it. Third, ethnicity has developed to a great extent, especially amongst larger minorities. Finally, Britain has always been a racist state.

Selected documents

Document 1

Joe Jacobs, *Out of the Ghetto: My Youth in the East End*, London, 1978, p. 11, describing the origins of his parents.

My parents arrived within a couple of years of each other at the turn of the century. Mother was born in Kodish, Poland in 1877. My father, who was much older, came from Kiev in Russia. He left behind a wife, three sons and a daughter. My mother had one daughter from her first husband who had been conscripted in Poland and had deserted my mother in the process. She came to London to join her two sisters and their families who arrived here a little earlier. A younger sister and husband followed later.

Document 2

Creslaw, a Polish soldier, describing his movement to England at the start of 1945. Reprinted from: Ethnic Communities Oral History Project, *Passport to Exile: The Polish Way to London*, London, 1988, pp. 20–1.

The outbreak of the war affected my family very much. When the Russians came in 1939 we hardly had any food at home. We tried to survive, Father tried his best. It was not very safe for me to stay at home because the Russians tried to get me, they wanted to take me to Russia to educate me. I was against this, I didn't want education from the Russians, no way. I was supposed to go to Moscow to be educated but I went to the forest.

The Jerries attacked the Russians in June 1941 on June 21st and the Germans caught me, I go from one hands to the other and that's it. They kept me in my home town for about three or four weeks, I escaped from there and they got me again. Then they take me to Lithuania, I was there for four months, I was in a big camp. It was very bad, no food, the food was terrible, people were dying of hunger. They took me to Germany, I had no way out, I had to eat raw potatoes and grass to survive. I escaped two times from Germany. Four of my friends from my home town were killed and I came out alive. There were many times in my life when I thought I was going to die, I've seen death many times and I can't get out of that.

The first time I was working in a steel mine and I escaped from there and I was in France for one month. For four weeks I was free, I was free but I had nothing to eat. I tried not to get into trouble but the Germans caught me again, beat me up and put me back to camp. They told me they were going to execute me then, shoot me. I said why not shoot me, shoot me now, they didn't. I waited until I had a chance when they took us to Luxembourg by train, so I jumped out of the train. That was the only way out − to jump out of the train, to survive or die. All my friends died because the Americans bombed that train. They thought they were transporting the German Army but the only Germans were on top of the coal wagons, they smashed the lot but I jumped out before that.

Then I went to France, back to France. A German soldier came to me and spoke fluent Polish and said to me 'Get out,' the war wasn't far he said 'Get out or you'll be shot,' they set fire to the village. I ran to the forest but you know when somebody is chasing you you have no strength to run, but I did get out and after that I went to a Russian camp. I told them I was Russian, I told them where I came from in Russia, I spoke Russian. I was given plenty food, cigarettes, plenty to drink. I stayed there about three weeks, after that I saw two Americans and a Polish officer, they said 'any Polish people step forward'. Only I stepped forward and everybody looked at me because I had said I was Russian. So I went and joined the Polish Army in France. I joined the army and from there, there were a lot of us, it took two big ships to transport us to England.

Document 3

Extract from an article entitled 'How the Jews are Expelled', published in *Darkest Russia*, 15 July 1891, an English newspaper concerned with the plight of Jews in Russia.

In March a Commission was appointed to make a searching inquiry concerning the Jews residing in the environs of Moscow, to ascertain whether they were actually engaged in their trades and were *bona fide* artisans. This commission proceeded in an extraordinary manner, to discover who were actually working and who were unoccupied. It had already been decided that any artisan found unemployed was to be virtually expelled.

The members of the Commission merely stationed themselves outside the houses of Jews, entered the names of all the inhabitants, and pronounced the majority of them to be unemployed, making exception only in rare instances. A certain Jewish tailor seeing the iniquities outside his dwelling place hastened out, and implored them to enter his abode, to see the number of workmen employed there, and then to declare them as actively engaged at their trades. They refused his request, and added his name to the list of those deserving expulsion.

In Moscow proper, inquisitional raids are made suddenly by night on the houses of well-known families – those of physicians, lawyers, apothecaries, etc. Between one and two a.m. they prosecute a most careful search in all the rooms, in the bedrooms of married and unmarried women. The latter are disturbed so that it may be seen whether they have concealed in their apartments those who, by the new laws, have been deprived of the right to remain in the city.

When the work of the Commission concerning the environs of Moscow was ended, the Governor was authorised to expel some five hundred families from the Moscow district. They left a few in the neighbourhood to make it appear that the expulsion was based on the inquiries made, but those now privileged to remain will, before long, be expelled like the rest.

Document 4

Origins of Germans assisted by the Society of Friends of Foreigners in Distress for selected years

Area of origin	Number and year in which assisted		
	1865–6	1877–8	1883
Baden	44	38	19
Bavaria	81	71	32
Hesse	440	327	24
Hanover	222	–	–
Hanse cities	106	63	47
Mecklenburg	12	9	–
Nassau	112	–	2
Oldenburg	2	1	–
Prussia	703	1,569	454
Saxony	42	16	47
Württemberg	33	55	28
Other states	76	2	–

Source: Society of Friends of Foreigners in Distress, *An Account of the Society of Friends of Foreigners in Distress for the Year 1866*, London, 1866, p. 33; Bremen Staatsarchiv, 2 T 6 t 4 d, 'An Account of the Society of Friends of Foreigners in Distress for the Year 1878'; *Londoner Courier*, 6 February 1884.

Document 5

An interview held by the Select Committee on Emigration and Immigration (Foreigners), *Parliamentary Papers*, vol. XI, 1888, pp. 69–70.

ABRAM FRANCOISE, called in; and examined through an interpreter.

Chairman.

1427. Where do you come from? – Three Rusian Miles from Memel, about 12 English miles, on the Russian side of Memel.

1428. What were you doing there? – I have been a shoemaker, but now am old, and cannot work.

1429. What made you come to England? – I was very anxious to marry a daughter of mine, but I had no dowry for her, and someone wrote and said that if she came over and learnt some trade, she might be able to save sufficient to have a dowry.

1430. Have you brought your daughter to this country? – Yes, and she is learning button-hole making.

1431. Who wrote and asked you to come? – Some of my countrymen.
1432. Someone wrote from London telling you that your daughter might earn money here? – That she might be able to earn enough here to be able to get a dowry?
1433. Have you got your passage ticket? – Yes.
1434. Where are you living now? – I do not really know the name but it is somewhere in the neighbourhood of Brick-lane.

Document 6

Eduardo Martinez, a Basque refugee child, describing his early days in England. Reprinted from: Ethnic Communities Oral History Project, *Ship of Hope*, London, 1991, pp. 8–9.

When we originally came here we were all taken to Southampton, in Eastleigh, near Southampton and we were in camps there. We were all either Nationalists, or Anarchists or Communists or Socialists or whatever. We were all separated into groups. I didn't know anything about this at the time.

It didn't matter how old you were. In fact that was the terrible thing about it. I came with my elder sister, she was 15, and at the beginning they separated you on your parents' belief at the time, and that's how you were labelled, in fact we were all separated into different sections like that and as regards my sister and me we were separated because she was a girl and I was a boy. Although I was just six years old that didn't have any bearing at all, we were just put in tents, put outside and that was it.

Well, my father was Communist, had been from the Communist Party, so I was automatically put in that section. But at the time I didn't know anything about it except of course afterwards that we were all either supposed to be Anarchists or Nationalists or Socialists or whatever, you know that's all that really mattered then.

In Southampton, in Eastleigh, I remember queuing for food, and I remember the music that they had to play to wake us up in the morning over the tannoy. That kind of thing is very, very vivid indeed. We lived in tents, the one that I used to be in was about eight or so to a tent. They were reasonably sized tents.

In Southampton there was many people when we first came over, about 5,000, it was really too big and too impersonal. I didn't know anybody, quite frankly. I came with my sister but we were separated immediately we came off the boat, and quite frankly I hardly saw her at all, in fact I don't recall if I ever saw her in Southampton. I don't even know how long we were there but I have a feeling it must have been something like two months.

Some people started leaving earlier than others. Some people stayed much longer. From there we went to what I think must have been a transition camp, I don't know because we were only there for two weeks and it was in army sheds. It must have been somewhere around Surrey because afterwards we were taken to Bray Court, which was the first colony that I really remember at all. Bray Court was near Maidenhead. I do remember we were there for some months. This was quite a biggish colony. We were in a house that used to be at a hotel at one time, with very imposing grounds and all that. It was very, very nice indeed. We were there about six months, in Bray Court. It was a mixed colony and I was there with my sister. We both went to that colony and they used to organise concerts from there and my sister used to be in the dancing group. They used to give concerts in different places and once they went to Belfast and my sister in fact stayed there, in Belfast. She was adopted there and subsequently a little bit later she took me over there and I spent two years in Belfast.

Document 7

The following gives details about the formation of a local committee to receive refugee children from Germany. Reprinted from: K. Gershon, *We Came as Children: A Collective Autobiography*, London, 1966, p. 42.

Our local Committee for the Care of Refugee Children from Germany was formed early in December 1938. Letters from the Mayor asking for help appeared in the local Press for several weeks, and there was an immediate response in the form of donations, invitations, and offers of education.

From the beginning the Committee concentrated on requests for offers of hospitality for the children in private homes, either free or with a maintenance grant, which was fixed at the rate of 12s. 6d weekly, the normal amount paid for boarded out children in England. They resolved not to found Hostels for the children unless other means failed, realising that true home life was the necessity for happiness, and that the best interests of the children would be served by helping them to merge into the population as British citizens, rather than to isolate them in little foreign colonies.

Document 8

John Denvir, *The Irish in Britain*, London, 1892, pp. 392–3, giving an account of Irish communities in London.

The Irish are numerous in Clerkenwell . . . South Hackney, Bethnal

Green, and Haggerston are noted centres of the boot and shoemaking trade, which gives employment to a portion of the Irish population in these districts. In Marylebone, North Kensington, Chelsea, Fulham and Westminster, these are districts where the Irish and their descendants are largely in evidence. As in other parts of London, while there is a satisfactory proportion who have 'got on', the bulk of these are in the ranks of labour. It is satisfactory to know that many Irish labourers in connection with the building trades have been able to bring up their sons as masons, carpenters, or bricklayers. Among the artisan class you find many who have received a fair education at the schools in connection with the various Catholic churches – men who have never, perhaps, seen Ireland but who are among the staunchest upholders of the national cause, as well as being the keenest and most intelligent politicians to be found in the metropolis.

On the south side of the Thames you find small colonies of our people in Camberwell, Peckham, and other centres. In fact they are everywhere – even in places where you never dream of finding them, as any priest will tell you who has ever opened a mission in London . . .

Perhaps the densest mass of Irish is to be found among the river-side population stretching for miles eastward of London Bridge, on both sides of the Thames. On the north side you meet them in large numbers in Whitechapel, Wapping, Shadwell, Limehouse, Poplar, Millwall, Barking Road and Silvertown, their chief employment being in connection with shipping . . . On the north side of the Thames the Irish population is largest in Southwark, Bermondsey, Rotherhithe, and Deptford, and mostly employed at the docks and the river-side. In and about Bermondsey you find a number of them connected with various branches of the leather trade, for which the district is noted, both as employers and work people.

Document 9

Leon M. Faucher, *Manchester in 1844: its Present Condition and Future Prospects*, London, 1844, pp. 28–30, describing the Irish population of Manchester.

For several years the Irish labourers formed the most abject portion of the population, their dwellings were the most dirty and un-healthy, and their children the most neglected. It was in the cellars occupied by them that the illicit distillation of ardent spirits was carried on. Misery of every description, fever, roguery, debauchery, and theft, were rife amongst them; their neighbourhood was the chosen retreat of vagabonds and criminals, scarcely a day passed without some disturbance or without some serious crime.

Happily, however, these features of the Irish population have undergone a remarkable change.

Document 10

Article from the Irish *Nation* of 14 June 1856 in a series on 'The Irish in England' entitled 'The Iron Country'.

> Within some miles or so of Birmingham stands the town of West Bromwich: near at hand is Oldbury; within their precincts some five or six hundred Irish have sought and received 'leave to toil'. Here, however severe the hardships of the first immigrants might have been, the traces of the struggle are less marked than in Darlaston and Wednesbury. A good church of spacious dimensions gives evidence of a zealous pastor and a large and attentive congregation . . .
>
> In this district . . . the Irish are employed at those laborious tasks that require great physical strength more than skill; charging or cleaning out the blast furnaces, removing the slag, &c.

Document 11

Extract from an article by George R. Sims in the *Strand Magazine*, vol. 29, 1905, pp. 510–11, entitled 'Round Little Italy'.

> The strange and, by all things considered, picturesque colony of Italian peasants in the heart of London is called 'Little Italy' by its own inhabitants, and though described as in Clerkenwell it is, as a matter of fact, situated principally in Holborn. Two iron posts at the bottom of Eyre Street Hill mark the spot where Holborn ends and Clerkenwell begins. The old boundary was the Fleet Ditch, which is now covered in and rarely asserts itself here, as it does occasionally nearer the Thames . . .
>
> Sunday morning is the best time to make the Little Italian trip, because not only are most of the inhabitants at home, but the poor Italians scattered about in other parts of London make the main street of the colony their rendezvous . . .
>
> There is a general idea that the distinguishing features of Little Italy are poverty and dirt. I have even seen it stated in print that it is not a safe place for the stranger. It will astonish many to learn that the Italian quarter, the home of the organ-grinders and the ice-cream and roast-chestnut venders, is clean and well-ordered, and that it is

under far better sanitary control than many districts of London in which the dreaded alien immigrant has found no foothold.

Let us visit it first on Sunday morning. The main street is filled with a lounging crowd. At the tops of the courts groups are gathered together in animated conversation. Many of the men are models of virile symmetry, and the children are clean, well-dressed, and good-looking. In the streets that lie off the main thoroughfare there are houses painted in bright colours in the Italian style, and when the window of one of these opens and an Italian woman in her native head-dress looks out the eye of the artist is charmed. London has vanished. It is a spring morning in some southern Italian town. The people may be poor, but the note of squalor which makes our English poverty so terrible is not to be found here. The men and women who stroll about the streets or gather at the corners have inherited the proud carriage and the clean-cut features of the citizens of the great Italian States. Here in Little Italy the Romans of Michael Angelo, the venetians of Titian, the Florentines of Raphael walk again.

Document 12

An extract on the living conditions of the Irish in England from the Royal Commission on the Condition of the Poorer Classes in Ireland, Appendix G, The State of the Irish Poor in Great Britain, *Parliamentary Papers*, vol. 34, 1836, p. xi.

In all the towns of England and Scotland where the Irish have settled, they inhabit the *cheapest* dwellings which can be procured; and thus they are collected in the lowest, dampest, dirtiest, most unhealthy, and ruinous parts of the town. In Liverpool and Manchester very many of them inhabit cellars, which are frequently dark, confined and wet. In Scotch towns there are not many inhabited cellars; but the rooms in the narrow closes of Glasgow, Edinburgh, and Greenock are darker and smaller, apparently less fitted for the residence of human beings, than even the cellars of the large towns of Lancashire. In these dwellings, an Irish family usually occupies a room, or at most two rooms; and frequently, in addition to their own numbers, they take in a single man or woman, or a widow with children or lodgers. It rarely happens that they rent an entire house or cottage. They have likewise a practice, to a great extent, of living in lodging houses, in which single beds are let by the week or by the night, and large numbers are crowded together in the same room. The state of these houses is usually wretched in the extreme; and, from the filthy condition of the bedding, the want of the commonest articles of furniture, and the uncleanly habits of the inmates themselves, and the numbers which, without distinction of age and sex, are closely crowded together, they are frequently the means of generating and communicating infectious diseases.

Document 13

An extract from 'The London Irish', *Blackwood's Edinburgh Magazine*, vol. 170, 1901, pp. 125–6.

The bulk of the race lives in typical working-class neighbourhoods, such as the East End, and the very poor part of South London between Blackfriars and London Bridges, or in the worst slums of all, those that jostle wealth, such as Drury Lane, corners in Chelsea (off Pelham Crescent and Sidney Street) and Notting Hill, and whole streets in Shepherd's Bush and Kensal Town. Unskilled and casual labour supports them, for the most part – work demanding little more than a brawny arm and a square pair of shoulders. That is a true London proverb, that poverty and gasworks go together. Those unsightly establishments employ large numbers of Irishmen, and the managers complain of their unfitness for work on Monday mornings. The railways, too, especially the lines running southwards, have many Irishmen in their pay, and superintendents have told us that for a few hours' exertion at high pressure Irish navvies have no superiors.

Document 14

R. H. Sherard, *The White Slaves of England*, London, 1897, pp. 128–30, commenting on Jewish tailors in Leeds.

But from what I saw in the sweating dens in the Leylands, I am convinced that their circumstances are, at least, as bad as those of the sweated tailors in London. They all work on a weekly wage, and from twelve to seventeen hours a day. Here may be seen, in some filthy room in an old dilapidated factory in the Leylands, fifty people (men, women, boys, and girls), all huddled together, sewing as though for dear life. A girl may be earning 6s a week, a man from 22s to 30s. The stench in the room, its uncleanliness, surpass description. The finished garments are lying pell-mell on the floor in the filth and the vermin.

They are 'flogged into their work', as one said, 'for all the time the gaunt sweater stalks about, scolding, inspecting, while now and then he will snatch a garment from some worker's hand, and set himself to work upon it, whilst a stream of vituperation pours from his lips. He is usually a haggard and starveling man, himself a victim of inhuman competition. There are weeks when he does not earn a penny for himself. In a good week he may earn 10*l*. The Jews work almost exclusively on men's and youth's coats. They do no cutting, and they seem unable to make 'juveniles' and 'trouserings'.

Document 15

James Greenwood, *The Wilds of London*, London, 1874, pp. 265–6, on conditions in a German sugar refinery in the East End of London, which he had just entered.

It was a sort of handy outer warehouse, that to which we were first introduced – a low-roofed, dismal place with grated windows, and here and there a foggy little gas-jet burning blear-eyed against the wall. The walls were black – not painted black. As far as one might judge they were bare brick, but, "basted" unceasingly by the luscious steam that enveloped the place, they had become coated with a thick preserve of sugar and grime. The floor was black, and all corrugated and hard, like a public thoroughfare after a shower and then a frost. The roof was black, and pendent from the great supporting posts and balks of timber were sooty, glistening icicles and exudings like those of the gum-tree. 'Sugar, sugar everywhere, but not a bit to eat.' Exactly the Bogeydom to which should be consigned for a term, according to the degree of their iniquity, the owners of larcenous little fingers so persistent in their attacks on the domestic sugar-basin. At the extremity of this gloomy cave, and glowing duskily at the mouth of a narrow passage, was dimly visible a gigantic globular structure in a bright copper, and hovering about it a creature with bare arms and chest all grizzly-haired, with a long bright rod of iron in his grasp, which incessantly he waved about the mighty caldron; this was doubtless the Sugar Ogre himself, in waiting for juvenile delinquents.

Document 16

Henry Mayhew, *London Labour and the London Poor*, vol. 4, 1861–2, reprinted London, 1968, pp. 419–20, on 'The French Beggar'.

My reader has most likely, in a quiet street, met a shabby little man, who stares about him in a confused manner, as if he had lost his way. As soon as he sees a decently dressed person he shuffles up to him, and taking off a 'casquette' with considerably more brim than body, makes a slight bow, and says in plaintive voice, 'Parlez Français, m'sieu?'

If you stop and, in an unguarded moment, answer 'Oui,' the beggar takes from his breast-pocket a greasy leather book, from which he extracts a piece of carefully folded paper, which he hands you with a pathetic shrug.

The paper, when opened, contains a small slip, on which is written in a light, foreign hand –

'You are requested to direct the bearer to the place to which he desires to go, as he cannot speak English!'

The beggar then, with a profusion of bows, points to the larger paper.

'Mais, m'sieu, ayez la bonté de lire. C'est Anglais.'

The larger paper contains a statement in French and English, that the bearer Jean Baptiste Dupont is a native of Troyes, Champagne, and a fan-maker by trade: that paralysis in the hand has deprived him of the power of working; that he came to England to find a daughter, who had married an Englishman and was dwelling in Westminster, but that when he arrived he found they had parted for Australia; that he is fifty-two years of age, and is a deserving object of affection, having no means of returning to Troyes, being an entire stranger to England, and having no acquaintances or friends to assist him.

This statement is without any signature, but no sooner have you read it than the beggar, who would seem to have a blind credence in the efficacy of documents, draws from his pocket-book a certificate of birth, a register of marriage, a passport, and a permission to embark, which, being all in a state of crumpled greasiness, and printed and written in French, so startles and confounds the reader, that he drops something into the man's hand and passes on.

Document 17

Hugh Heinrick, *A Survey of the Irish in England*, London, 1872, reprinted 1990, pp. 92–3, on the religious activities of the Irish in Liverpool.

The religious and educational requirements of the Irish in Liverpool are very well attended to, and all that zeal and labour can effect for the safety and preservation of the people is done on their behalf. Here the Irish people have, in nearly every instance, furnished the means, and Irish priests and Irish teachers, following in the footsteps of the people, have been mainly instrumental in fostering the intelligence and preserving the faith of their countrymen. But whether furnished from English or Irish sources, the evidences that the Faith is vital and progressive, and that the means for the education of the people are not wanting, meet the eye at very turn. There are twenty-three Catholic churches, ten convents, and seven monasteries in Liverpool.

These have all, or nearly all, been built, and are now supported, by the zealous charity of the Irish people. The rich contribute their pound; the poor, their pence; and so churches and schools have risen in evidence of the constancy in faith and the loving thirst for mental cultivation which had ever distinguished the Irish people. The church accommodation – one church to 8,000 population – can scarcely be deemed sufficient; but the school accommodation is almost, if not entirely, equal to the requirements of the time. A careful examination of the School Board statistics will show that the Catholic population of Liverpool have provided school accommodation in elementary schools, industrial schools, and reformatories, for 22,369 children; or for about one in eight of the Catholic population – a proportion which in a community such as this, where a larger proportion of the people remain unmarried than in most other towns – is found to be ample for present requirements. These statistics only supply information in reference to schools within the borough. Outside this boundary there are several large schools, public and private. There is probably school accommodation in and around Liverpool for 25,000 children – certainly for a larger number, if we include Birkenhead and the smaller places on the other side of the Mersey.

Document 18

Attendance at German Church Services in London in 1905

Location	Attendance		
	Morning	Evening	Total
St George's, Stepney	166		166
St Paul's, Stepney	49	126	175
German YMCA, Stepney		29	29
German Seaman's Church, Stepney		11	11
German Sailor's Home, Stepney		34	34
Hamburg Lutheran, Hackney	86	132	218
Great Titchfield Street, Marylebone		34	34
Eccleston Street, Westminster	33		33
Fowler Road, Islington	119	58	177
Dacres Road, Forest Hill	138	58	196
High Street, Deptford		35	35
Windsor Road, Camberwell	57		57
Star Lane, West Ham	10	19	29
St Mary's, St Pancras	120	161	259
Leighton Crescent, St Pancras		47	47
Total	778	744	1,522

Source: Richard Mudie Smith, *Religious Life of the People in London*, London, 1905, pp. 52, 66, 99, 107, 173, 177, 235, 239, 243, 253.

Document 19

The Twenty-fifth Annual Report of the Mission among the German Poor in London, and the School in Connection with it, London, 1874, pp. 5–6, outlining objectives.

> The object of the Mission is twofold, first with regard to adults, to visit the poor in their houses, especially the sick, to offer them kind Christian advice and the comforts of the Word of God, to sell, lend, or distribute among them Christian books and Bibles, to gather them also in weekly Bible classes especially suited for the poor, and to induce them, if possible, to attend any of the German Protestant churches, and to lead a Christian life . . .
>
> The second object of the Mission embraces the education of the German poor, chiefly in the East of London, for which a day-school has been established now there twelve years in Leman-street, Whitechapel, which has been attended during the past year by from 150 to 200 children.

Document 20

Extract from an article in the *Illustrated London News*, 24 October 1863, entitled 'The King of the Greeks attending Divine Service at the Greek Church'.

> The small but important community of Greek merchants in London manifested their fidelity to George I, the newly-elected King of the Greeks, by causing a grand 'Te Deum' to be sung, on Sunday week, in honour of his Majesty, at the Greek Church, on London-wall, on which occasion the King honoured his subjects dwelling in London by his presence.
>
> The church is a small but well-built edifice in the Byzantine style, having a high vaulted roof. It was erected about twenty years ago by the Greek residents of London, who bought the ground and expended altogether about £20,000 on the work.

Document 21

F. M. Holmes, 'Some Foreign Places of Worship in London', in G. R. Sims (ed.), *Living London*, vol. 3, 1903, pp. 229–30, on a service in St Sophia's Greek Orthodox Church in London.

> From the flashing sunlight of a bright spring day we turn into the crowded church of St Sophia, Moscow Road, Bayswater. The

large congregation has risen to its feet. Priests, generously arrayed, advance from the richly painted altar-screen towards an open space under the dome. One, the Archimandrite, bears a lighted candle in his hand, while a sonorous voice proclaims in modern Greek, a sentence which may be thus interpreted:

> All come and take the light that never sets, and embrace Christ, Who has risen from the dead.

The second priest, and the lay-reader after him, light their candles at that of the Archimandrite, repeating the sonorous proclamation, and then persons from the congregation move forward, not in a hurried, disorderly rush, but quietly, one or two at a time, and light the tapers which they hold in their hands, at the larger candles borne by the priests. These individuals among the congregation in their turn allow their neighbours to do likewise, and thus the light is passed round the church to nearly everyone in the large and beautiful building.

It is the service of the Resurrection, celebrated on Easter Sunday in the Greek Church. The lighting of the candles is symbolic, and is said to represent the new light which came into the world with Christ – the new teaching of the Gospel.

The service proceeds. The choir sings superbly. The sonorous voice sounds frequently.

The crowded congregation – or by far the greater number – remains standing throughout, though the service lasts for nearly two hours. The dark southern faces appear very attentive, and the worshippers make the sign of the cross at frequent intervals. Some who might be Greek sailors, though dressed in their best, are here; others evidently are prosperous merchants. It is a festival service, the church is light and bright and ornate, the gleam of hundreds of candles shines on rich marbles, and during the morning the priest proclaims:

> If any be pious and a lover of God, let him enjoy this beautiful and bright festal gathering.

At the close, when the last notes of the choir have died away and the sonorous voices are heard no more, the priests make their way through the throng to tables by the main entrances, and there they distribute gaily coloured genuine Easter eggs to the crowds of worshippers according to ancient custom and as a sign of rejoicing.

Document 22

An extract from Count E. Armfelt, 'German London', in George R. Sims (ed.), *Living London*, vol. 3, 1903, pp. 60–1, describing the range of German clubs existing in London.

It has been said with truth that wherever a dozen Germans meet there is sure to be a *Verein* of some sort. The *Verein* is not a club, nor is it a union, as we understand these words, but it partakes of both and is something more besides.

Here, for instance, is the *Deutscher Turnverein* (the German Gymnastic Society), which imparts instruction in athletics, fencing, and boxing, and has its special days for signing-on. It is also a club, for it has its restaurant and its wine cellars. The fair sex is not neglected, for its dances are features of the Society. In the centre of London there is the *Deutscher Gewerbe und Theater Verein* (the German Industrial and Theatre Club). It caters also for families. Attached to it are the *Verein* of German Bicyclists and the *Verein* of Typographers and the Chess Club. On Saturdays there is a *Tanzkranzchen* (a dance gathering), a concert, and a dramatic recitation; while on Sundays about half-past five there is a *Schauspiel*, or drama, at the end of which dancing follows. On all occasions there is good eating and drinking at moderate prices. There is also a Benefit Society, which provides for the sick, the out-of-work, and the burial of the dead.

A number of these clubs also give facilities for the commercial and industrial training of their members and their instruction in the English language. The *Vereins* in the east and west are all very much alike. They provide for theatrical performances, dramatic recitals, dancing and singing, and all the usual social amusements for both sexes. At Yuletide in particular dances are arranged, when the Christmas-tree forms, of course, a very prominent feature. Moreover, there are rooms where billiards, chess, cards, and other games are played in the evening, and where eating and drinking are general at all hours. And each of these clubs, and many German public-houses, have their *Kegel-bahn*, or German skittle alley, which is well patronised . . .

But no description of German life, be it *Verein* life or home life, can be complete without reference to the *Lied*. Every *Verein* – the German Gymnasium included – has its *Lieder-Tafel*, its social gathering for song . . .

Besides the *Vereins*, whose membership is counted in thousands, there are all over London very small societies, which meet in rooms reserved for them in the German restaurants. Each society has its one or two evenings in the week, some for chorus singing, others for card-playing.

Document 23

Extract from Swiss Mercantile Society, *Annual Report, 1919–1920*,
London, 1920, p. 8, on the range of activities carried on by the
organisation.

Foremost of all we wish to comment here on the still tighter bond
of friendship existing within our own circle. For this our weekly
social gatherings every Thursday night are primarily responsible.
We can but favourably speak of the present existing arrangements
between the Union Helvetia Club and ourselves. A good number of
our members are therefore meeting regularly and enjoy the company
of friends, be it at a game of cards or skittles.

We have not escaped either that contagious dance fever which
was so prevalent in London immediately after the cessation of
hostilities, and at its height during last winter, and have therefore
five Cinderella Dances to record, which were all held at the Midland
Hotel, St Pancras, and splendidly arranged for, thanks to the care of
our Entertainment Committee, whose efforts might well have been
recompensed by a better than average attendance.

On different occasions we have had the opportunity of inviting as
our guests, representatives of our sister societies, whereas the SMS was
frequently represented on theirs. These mutual friendly representations
are indeed very significant of the good fellowship existing between the
constituent societies of the Swiss Colony, and which is making itself
more felt as beneficial to the unity of the colony.

Document 24

Membership card of the Jewish League for Woman Suffrage, 1913.

Objectives and Methods.

1. The JLWS is a non-party organisation formed to demand the
Parliamentary Franchise for women on the same terms as it is, or
may be, granted to men; and to unite Jewish Suffragists of all
shades of opinion for religious and educational activities.

2. The League will carry on propaganda on constitutional lines
parallel with those of the existing Church, Catholic, Free Church
and Friends' Leagues.

3. The League will emphasise the need for women's emancipation to secure the effective co-operation of men and women in
combating social evils.

4. The JLWS will strive to further the improvement of the status of women in the Community and the State.

Membership.

All Jewish men and women who are in sympathy with the objectives and methods are eligible for membership.

Document 25

An extract from the *Daily Telegraph*, 11 February 1909, reprinted in Correspondence between the Secretary of State for the Home Department and his Honour Judge Rentoul, KC, on the Subject of the Expulsion of Aliens, *Parliamentary Papers*, vol. LXX, 1909.

> Judge Rentoul, K. C., lecturing last night on 'The British Empire: Its Greatness, Glory and Freedom', at the Bishopsgate Institute Hall, in connection with the Guild of Freedom of the City of London, said he left the Old Bailey that afternoon at five o'clock, after sitting exactly a week. Three-fourths of the cases tried were those of aliens of the very worst type in their own country. He had in mind before him the Russian burglar, the Polish thief, the Italian stabber, and the German swindler. These people, in three cases, at any rate, were banished from their own country. Take the last case, tried a few hours previously – that of a man who had deserted the German Army. He was sought by the police, escaped, committed embezzlement in his own country, and began business here, with the result that he swindled several innocent people, and had now gone to be supported by the people of this country. (Cries of "Shame"!) In one single week these people had been before him – people whom this country would be glad to get rid of and who had been practically kicked out of their own. That was a state of affairs which concerned both political parties, and while it was all very well to talk about an open door for the political refugee, men who were known to the police as of bad character should not be allowed to enter the country. He was not railing against party government in politics, but in the matter of alien immigration Empire should be placed before party advantage.

Document 26

An extract from Paul Cohen-Portheim, *Time Stood Still: My Internment in England*, London, 1931, p. 85, commenting on the lack of privacy in his internment camp in Wakefield.

> There is nothing like it to be found anywhere else. Monks retire to their cells, soldiers have their days or weeks off; here it continues for ever, and the longer it continues the more you suffer from it. No privacy, no possibility of being alone, no possibility of finding *quietude*. It is inhuman, cruel and dreadful to force people to live in closest community for years; it becomes almost unbearable when the community is abnormally composed like that of a prisoners' camp. There are no women, no children, there is no old age and next to no youth there, there is just a casual rabble of men forced to be inseparable. Try to imagine – though it is impossible really to understand without having experienced it – what it means, *never* to be *alone* and *never* to know *quiet*, not for a minute, and to continue thus for years, and you will begin to wonder that there was no general outbreak of insanity, that there remained a difference between lunacy and barbed-wire nerves.

Document 27

William Cobbett's comments on Jews from his *Good Friday or the Murder of Jesus Christ by the Jews*, London, 1830, pp. 16–17.

> With regard to the TEMPORAL GOOD of a nation, what can be more pernicious than to give countenance and encouragement to a race, whose God is gain; who live by money-changing; who never labour in making, or causing to come, any thing useful to man; who are usurers by profession, and extortioners by habit and almost by instinct; who, to use the words of the prophet, carry on 'usury and increase, and greedily gain of their neighbours by extortion'? This propensity they appear to have in their very nature: it seems to be inborn with them to be continually drawing to themselves the good of all around them. In all the states, where they have been encouraged, they have first assisted to rob and enslave the poeple, and, in the end, to destroy the government. A neighbouring nation, which was, at last, plunged into all the horrors of anarchy, they were the agents in bringing into that state of misery, which finally produced the lamentable catastrophe. They every where are on the side of oppression, assisting tyranny in its fiscal extortions; and every where they are the bitter foes of the popular rights and liberties, which are not more necessary to the happiness of the people than to the stability and dignity of the sovereign power; because, as long as those rights are in force, there is no room for a full display of their

153

talent of accumulation: it is amongst masses of debt and misery that they thrive as birds and beasts of prey get fat in times of pestilence.

Document 28

Arnold White, *The Modern Jew*, London, 1899, p. xii, on what he views as the clannishness of Jews.

Each immigrant foreign Jew settling in this country joins, not the English community as the Huguenots and the Hollander refugees from the Roman Catholic prosecutions of the seventeenth century joined us, but a community proudly separate, racially distinct, and existing preferentially aloof. Members of this community for successive generations, except in rare instances, decline to intermarry with non-Jews, maintain a different Sabbath, consume a different food, and are tied to alien communities of their own race and faith in other lands by closer bonds than any that unite them to the country of their adoption. This Jewish island in the sea of English life is small to-day. Few trades, interests, or classes are so directly affected by it as to create misgiving in the public mind that a danger menacing to national life had begun in our midst, is growing, and must be abated if sinister consequences are to be avoided. There are two methods, and only two, in which the evil results of a Jewish imperium inside the English Empire can be obviated. It can be destroyed and its members expelled as was done in the thirteenth century in most countries in Europe, including England, and is likely to be done over again in France, before many years have passed, or the Jewish community, frankly recognising the peril that besets them, must review their conduct and heavily work for or against the process of absorption which in two generations made French Protestants of the day of Louis XIV an integral part of the English people.

Document 29

An extract from Joseph Banister, *England under the Jews*, London, 1901, pp. 36–7.

The Jews not only compose the most numerous and undesirable element among our foreign invaders, but are at the head of the various movements for bringing other obnoxious aliens into this country. The vile looking Italians one sees laying asphalt in our streets are imported by a conspiracy composed of Jews. The introduction of foreign women for immoral purposes is carried on, as is the white slave traffic everywhere, chiefly, if not entirely, by Jews.

The profitable business of importing Italian ice-cream vendors and organ-grinders is reported to be a Jewish monopoly. The attempt to introduce swarms of Chinese laundrymen into England was made by Jews and received its support chiefly from Jews, and Jew-controlled newspapers. The large numbers of foreign domestic servants in London have almost all been brought into this country by Jews. Some time ago a small riot occurred in Wales, caused by the introduction, by a company of Belgian Jews, of some hundreds of Italian coal-miners; and the Poles employed in the coal-mines of Scotland are said to be also Jew imported. The German waiters and porters who cringe for tips at so many of our principal hotels, and the cheap German clerks we hear so much about, are imported and nowadays employed almost entirely by Jew firms.

Document 30

Arnold White, *Efficiency and Empire*, London, 1901, p. 80, on the influence of wealthy Jews.

The influence of bad foreign Jews on bad smart society is so real a danger to the Empire that it would be miraculous that the Press had ignored it, but for the remorseless control exercised by society and by the Jews over the expression of public opinion hostile to them. The Anglophobe Press abroad is written mainly by foreign Jews. In numbers, in wealth, in power, and in subtle influence over the whole community, foreigners, both poor and rich, are increasing by leaps and bounds. Material success is as truly the goal of the smart foreign Jew as it was in the days when his ancestors worshipped the calf of gold. Material success has never yet become the British ideal. These German Jews, who have already captured rather than earned so large a part of the good things going in England, despise the smart society they use as instruments of advancement. This island of aliens in the sea of English life is small to-day. It is growing rule by foreign Jews that is being set up. The best forms of our national life are already in jeopardy.

Document 31

Simon Laing, *Observations on the Social and Political State of the European People in 1848 and 1849*, London, 1850, p. 378, commenting upon the manners of Germans.

The manners . . . of all classes in Germany are so nearly the same, that there is no incongruity in their sitting together. All, from the prince to the shoemaker, are what our dainty gentry would call slovenly livers, dirty feeders, and insensible to the disgust they may give by habits confined, among us, to our lowest and most roughly bred classes. Spitting all round a room, picking their teeth at meals with the knife, licking it and thrusting it into the butter or cheese, and such petty abominations, show that there is not that marked difference in those small observances of delicacy, and of regard for the feelings of others, in manners and behaviour, which distinguish the gentleman from the non-gentleman in our population.

Document 32

An extract from W. Winwood Reade, *Savage Africa*, London, 1863, pp. 554–5, in which the author presents his impressions of Africans.

The typical negroes dwell in petty tribes, where all are equal, except the women, who are slaves; where property is common, and where, consequently, there is no property at all; where one may recognise the Utopia of philosophers, and observe the saddest and basest spectacles which humanity can afford.

The typical negro, unrestrained by moral laws, spends his days in sloth, his nights in debauchery. He smokes hashish till he stupefies his senses, or falls into convulsions; he drinks palm-wine till he brings on a loathsome disease; he abuses children; stabs the poor brute of a woman whose hands keep him from starvation; and makes a trade of his own offspring. He swallows up his youth in premature vice; he lingers through a manhood of disease; and his tardy death is hastened by those who no longer care to find him food.

Document 33

John Crawford, 'On the Physical and Mental Characteristics of the Negro', *Transactions of the Ethnological Society of London*, vol. 4, 1866, p. 212.

By the term Negro – in so far, at least, as it is applicable to Africa – we understand a human being with the hair of the head and other parts of the body always black, and more or less of the texture of wool, with a black skin of various shades; dark eyes, a flat face, depressed nose, jutting jaws, thick lips and large mouth, with oblique incisor teeth. To this is to be added a peculiar odour of the skin, offensive to and unknown in other races of man. The form of the skull, in so far as it is the brain-case, cannot, I think, be insisted on as a criterion of the African Negro, for I do not believe it has any characters by which it can certainly be distinguished from the skulls of nearly-allied races, such as those of the Abyssinians and of the Oriental Negroes. The true African Negro is of the average stature of Europeans, and perhaps even of their average physical strength; and in this last quality is the only race of man that is so.

Document 34

An extract from an antisemitic article in *Blackshirt*, 13 October 1936.

The first thing to note in fighting the great Jewish interest which controls much of our national life is that the big Jews are not fools. That is why they invariably win when they are only opposed by fools. On the contrary, when they are opposed by men cleverer and more determined than themselves, in the end they always lose. That is why Jews lost in Germany. That is why the British Union alone has established a nation-wide Movement in this country in the face of the Jewish attack. Small antisemitic societies have abounded in this country for years past. They have never obtained more than a handful of members and they have all failed. In fact, the Jews have won. The reason is that the Jews were much cleverer than they were.

Document 35

An extract from *The Times*, 13 May 1915, describing anti-German riots in east London.

There was very little work done in the East-end throughout the day. Shopkeepers of unequivocal British birth in the areas where rioting was most violent thought it wise to close their doors for the day, and in some of the streets which run off the Commercial-road there was scarcely a shop which was not shuttered.

The damage done by the rioters was very great. Not content with smashing doors and windows and looting the whole of the furniture and the contents of the shops, the interiors of the houses were in numerous instances greatly damaged. Staircases were hacked to pieces and ceilings were knocked down. Shops were completely wrecked before the police had time to arrive on the scene. At Poplar, for instance, in an area of a quarter of a mile half a dozen houses were attacked simultaneously by different crowds in the early afternoon. Before the constables were able to attempt to disperse the mob, horse-drawn carts, handcarts, and perambulators – besides the unaided arms of men, women, and children – had taken everything away from the wrecked houses. One saw pianos, chests of drawers, dressers, and the heaviest type of household furniture being carted triumphantly through the streets. 'Here is wealth for the taking,' said one man who had possession of several spring mattresses, and was calmly driving his overloaded donkey-cart down Crisp-street.

Document 36

A letter from the Chief Constable of Leeds, 18 June 1917, to the Home Office, on anti-Jewish riots in his city. From P[ublic] R[ecord] O[ffice], H[ome] O[ffice] 45 10810/311932.

With regard to the disturbances which occurred on Sunday evening, the 3rd inst., these commenced about 7–30 p.m. in the Jewish quarters, viz, The Leylands, when a large number of women and boys commenced to break the windows in the shops occupied by the Jews . . .

On Monday, the 4th instant, expecting that the disturbances would be renewed, I made arrangements for a large number of regular Police, augmented by a large number of the voluntary force of the Special Constabulary, to be located in various parts of the city. The disturbances were repeated about 7 p.m. and a large number of arrests were made, chiefly of boys, youths and females, and with the exception of one case – that of a woman charged with inflicting grievous bodily harm upon one of my Detective Inspectors – they were all dealt with by the Stipendiary Magistrate, Mr Horace Marshall, the following day.

I continued to keep up the reserve Police, prepared to deal with any further disorder, but I am pleased to inform you that no further outbreaks have taken place.

Select bibliography

Alderman, Geoffrey, *Modern British Jewry*, Oxford, 1992.

Alderman, Geoffrey, and Holmes, Colin (eds), *Outsiders and Outcasts: Essays in Honour of William J. Fishman*, London, 1993.

Ashton, Rosemary, *Little Germany: Exile and Asylum in Victorian England*, Oxford, 1986.

Baines, Dudley, *Emigration from Europe, 1815–1930*, London, 1991.

Buckman, Joseph, *Immigrants and the Class Struggle: The Jewish Immigrant Community in Leeds, 1880–1914*, Manchester, 1983.

Cahalan, Peter, *Belgian Refugee Relief in England during the Great War*, New York, 1982.

Cesarani, David (ed.), *The Making of Modern Anglo-Jewry*, Oxford, 1990.

Collins, Brenda, 'Proto-industrialisation and pre-Famine Emigration', *Social History*, vol. 7, 1982, 127–46.

Colpi, Terri, *The Italian Factor: The Italian Community in Great Britain*, Edinburgh, 1991.

Davis, Graham, *The Irish in Britain, 1815–1914*, Dublin, 1991.

Devine, T. M. (ed.), *Irish Immigrants and Scottish Cities in the Nineteenth and Twentieth Centuries*, Edinburgh, 1991.

Endelman, Todd M., *Radical Assimilation in English Jewish History, 1656–1945*, Bloomington, Indiana, 1990.

Finnegan, Frances, *Poverty and Prejudice: A Study of Irish Immigrants in York, 1840–1875*, Cork, 1982.

Fitzpatrick, David, '"A Peculiar Tramping People": the Irish in Britain, 1801–70', in W. E. Vaughan (ed.), *A New History of Ireland*, vol. 5, Oxford, 1989.

Fryer, Peter, *Staying Power: The History of Black People in Britain*, London, 1984.

Gainer, Bernard, *The Alien Invasion: The Origins of the Aliens Act of 1905*, London, 1972.

Garrard, John A., *The English and Immigration, 1880–1910*, Oxford, 1971.

Gartner, L. P., *The Jewish Immigrant in England, 1870–1914*, London, 1960.

Handley, J. E., *The Irish in Scotland, 1798–1845*, Cork, 1943.

Handley, J. E., *The Irish in Modern Scotland*, Cork, 1947.

Hirschfeld, Gerhard (ed.), *Exile in Great Britain: Refugees from Hitler's Germany*, Leamington Spa, 1984.

Holmes, Colin (ed.), *Immigrants and Minorities in British Society*, London, 1978.

Holmes, Colin, *Anti-semitism in British Society, 1876–1939*, London, 1979.

Holmes, Colin, *John Bull's Island: Immigration and British Society, 1871–1971*, London, 1988.

Hughes, Colin, *Lime, Lemon and Sarsaparilla: The Italian Community in South Wales, 1881–1945*, Bridgend, 1991.

Jackson, J. A., *The Irish in Britain*, London, 1963.

Jones, Douglas, 'The Chinese in Britain: Origins and Development of a Community', *New Community*, vol. 11, 1979.

Kushner, Tony, *The Persistence of Prejudice: Antisemitism in British Society during the Second World War*, Manchester, 1989.

Lebzelter, Gisela C., *Political Anti-semitism in England, 1918–1939*, New York, 1978.

Lees, Lynn Hollen, *Exiles of Erin: Irish Immigrants in Victorian London*, Manchester, 1979.

Lipman, V. D., *A Social History of the Jews in England*, London, 1954.

Lipman, V. D., *A History of the Jews in Britain since 1858*, Leicester, 1990.

Mayall, David, *Gypsy-Travellers in Nineteenth Century Society*, Cambridge, 1988.

Mayhew, Henry, *London Labour and the London Poor*, 4 volumes, 1861–2, London, 1968 reprint.

Mosse, Werner E. *et al.* (eds), *Second Chance: Two Centuries of German-speaking Jews in the United Kingdom*, Tübingen, 1991.

Neal, Frank, *Sectarian Violence: The Liverpool Experience, 1819–1914*, Manchester, 1988.

Ng, K. C., *The Chinese in London*, London, 1968.

O'Connor, Kevin, *The Irish in Britain*, Dublin, 1974.

OTuataigh, M. A. G., 'The Irish in Nineteenth Century Britain: Problems of Integration', *Transactions of the Royal Historical Society*, 5th series, vol. 31.

Panayi, Panikos, *The Enemy in our Midst: Germans in Britain during the First World War*, Oxford, 1988.

Panayi, Panikos (ed.), *Racial Violence in Britain, 1840–1950*, Leicester, 1993.

Panayi, Panikos, 'Refugees in Twentieth Century Britain: A Brief History', in Vaughan Robinson (ed.), *The International Refugee Crisis: British and Canadian Responses*, London, 1993.

Porter, Bernard, *The Refugee Question in Mid-Victorian Politics*, Cambridge, 1979.

Scobie, Edward, *Black Britannia: A History of Blacks in Britain*, Chicago, 1972.

Sims, George R. (ed.), *Living London*, 3 vols, London, 1902–3.

Sponza, Lucio, *Italian Immigrants in Nineteenth Century Britain: Realities and Images*, Leicester, 1988.

Swift, Roger, and Gilley, Sheridan (eds), *The Irish in the Victorian City*, London, 1985.

Swift, Roger, and Gilley, Sheridan (eds), *The Irish in Britain, 1815–1939*, London, 1989.

Thurlow, Richard, *Fascism in Britain: A History, 1918–1985*, Oxford, 1987.

Visram, Rozina, *Ayahs, Lascars and Princes: The Story of Indians in Britain, 1700–1947*, London, 1986.

Walvin, James, *Black and White: The Negro and English Society, 1555–1945*, London, 1973.

Wasserstein, Bernard, *Britain and the Jews of Europe, 1939–1945*, Oxford, 1988.

Watson, J. L., (ed.), *Between Two Cultures: Immigrants and Minorities in Britain*, Oxford, 1977.

Williams, Bill, *The Making of Manchester Jewry, 1740–1875*, Manchester, 1985 reprint.

Index